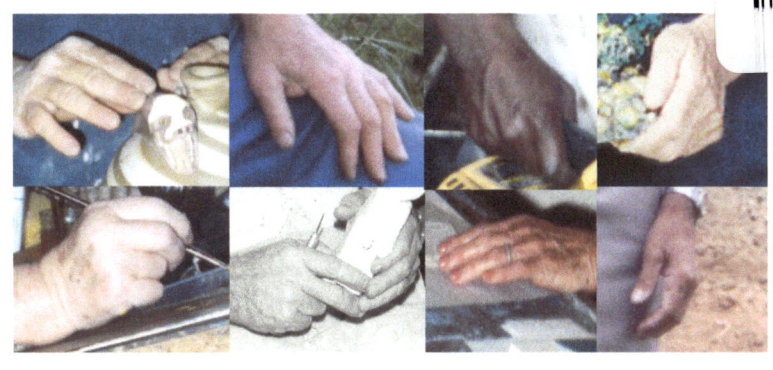

HAND-IN-HAND:

VISIONS & VOICES OF NORTH CAROLINA FOLK ARTISTS

BY

BARRY GURLEY HUFFMAN

PHOTOGRAPHY BY

ALLEN W. HUFFMAN, JR.

DEDICATED TO

MINNIE REINHARDT

(1898 – 1986)

A WONDERFUL LADY, MENTOR AND FRIEND

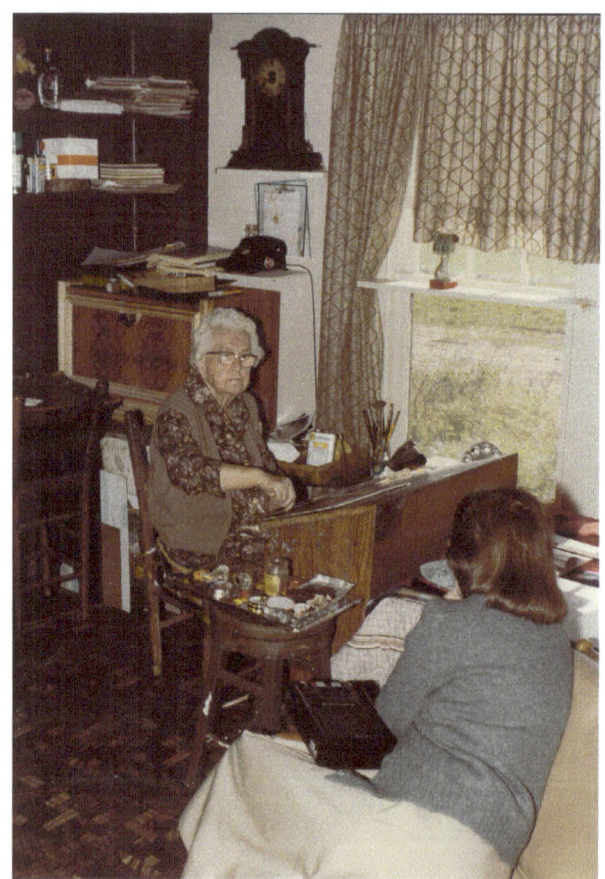

Author interviews Mrs. Reinhardt

COVER IMAGE
1991 painting by Barry Huffman of Minnie Reinhardt at work

THE LANGUAGE OF CANAAN

If dawn caught and dazzled on
dew beads strung to spider's web,
sweep of shadow crossed meadow
like a calming hand, it might come—luxuriant
bloom of assurance
grafted onto tongue, language
graced with a cadence so pure
ears deaf a lifetime now heard,
and for decades afterward
whole settlements would visit
streamside, meadow, that place one
world bled into another.

Ron Rash
Among the Believers

Acknowledgements

My deepest thanks goes

- ✌ to the artists who told me their stories,
- ✌ to Ardath Weaver who believed three decades did not diminish the value of these words and who encouraged me and labored to bring them to the printed page,
- ✌ to the North Carolina Arts Council,
- ✌ and to Allen, husband, photographer and fellow folk art traveler.

Recommendations

Visit the Hickory Museum of Art, Hickory, NC,
to see the Discover Folk Art exhibition and collection.

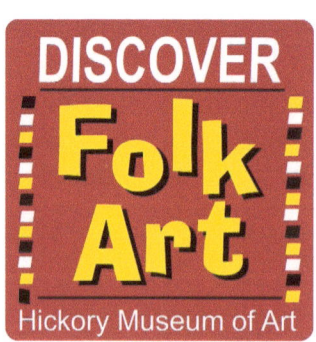

View The Memory Paintings of Minnie Reinhardt, produced by the Hickory Museum of Art, 1996, on You Tube at https://www.youtube.com/watch?v=n5jJSV22KAU

Book design: Ardath Goldstein Weaver

Preface: Timely Folk Art

The interviews in this book mark a place in time. In 1983, five years after we bought our first Minnie Reinhardt painting, I decided to record interviews of folk artists we had visited multiple times. I transcribed the interviews as accurately as possible, trying to preserve their speech patterns which I found to be lovely, capturing the artists' sense of place. Even today, decades later, when I read their words, I hear their voices speaking to me. Their vernacular speech expresses their rural roots and helps our understanding of the lives they have led.

I am a student, without benefit of any formal art education, an observer of the events and people that shaped what I think of as contemporary Southern self-taught art — sometimes called Folk Art — a movement that gained recognition in the last quarter of the twentieth century in America. My focus is the work of North Carolina artists and craftsmen.

In 1983, Southern folk art was just beginning to attract public attention. Although a few self-taught artists had been recognized for their work as early as the 1930s, the interest in this work on a wider scale did not gain momentum until the 1970s. Essentially, that interest was a grassroots movement fueled by the few art dealers and collectors who were seeking the work because they recognized the vitality, the sheer energy, of art created by artists working without academic rules. The art was edgy, original, and frequently fun. Indeed, the art often projected a raw creativity.

I came to appreciate folk art as I discovered the history and material culture of the Catawba Valley in North Carolina. My journey began in the 1960s when my husband Allen and I began our young married life seeking inexpensive weekend trips from Chapel Hill, North Carolina, and discovered the eighteenth century architecture of Colonial Williamsburg in Virginia. Walking the streets, studying buildings and wandering through beautiful gardens, we developed analytical eyes for what would become life-long interests in all things artistic.

After Allen's three year military obligation took us to West Germany in 1972, we returned to his hometown of Hickory with our two children. Our free time in Germany had been spent in museums and travel, so we returned to North Carolina to explore our own region. We discovered the work of Burlon Craig, a traditional potter, and he sent us to his neighbor, Mrs. Minnie Reinhardt, a Catawba County memory painter. We were on our way to becoming folk art collectors.

Over the next thirty plus years we visited many self-taught artists across the South. The time we spent with the artists was the most important and personally valuable part of these experiences. I had started painting prior to our going to Europe, and I was very curious to see what artists were creating, how they used materials and tools, and where they found inspiration. Allen, an amateur photographer, recorded our visits and over the decades he amassed a wonderful photographic archive of the people we visited. We often returned to artists to see new work, allowing him to document their changing work as well as their home 'studios,' their families and life situations. Frequently, we left with a souvenir of the visit — art we purchased to decorate our home.

Time.

Time can be defined as a measure in which events can be ordered from the past through the present into the future. The nature of time is movement, a seamless journey from past into present where the future is almost immediately the past. In a busy world, time can move at dizzying speed until life throws up a barrier that slows our perceptions to a crawl while we digest change. When we are young we tend to live in moments of circumstance that we think will go on indefinitely, but change is inevitable.

Time passed and the interviews, transcribed from tape recorder to hand written pages to typed pages, resided in boxes in a closet. Parts of some escaped briefly to be used on labeling panels for an exhibition of Southern contemporary folk art at the Hickory Museum of Art. Visitors from the North Carolina Arts Council took notice and offered encouragement and help to ready the interviews for publication. After as much as three decades these interviews have found their way to the printed page.

In looking back to the time spent with these very talented artists, I am deeply grateful to have shared moments from their busy lives. Outwardly they appeared to be 'ordinary' people — often reticent about being considered 'out of the ordinary' or even 'artists' — but they have left us with evidence of their talents and their passions to create. The quality of their work should demand our close attention because our society can benefit from a better understanding of creativity: where it comes from, what sparks it, and what drives self-taught artists to present it to the public.

Now join me as we step back in time for a few moments — hear the voices of 'ordinary' people talking about their lives. Share their visions of a creative world.

Read. Listen.

Barry Gurley Huffman

September 26, 2015

CONTENTS

Preface: Timely Folk Art   v

Introduction   ix

Minnie Reinhardt — Artist   11

Raymond Coins — Rock and Wood Worker   19

James Cook — Woodcarver   27

Burlon Craig — Potter   37

Elenora Hamilton — Painter   47

Jeff Williams — Woodcarver and Sculptor   59

Q.J. Stephenson — Naturalist and Sculptor   67

Albert Hodge — Potter   75

About The Project   86

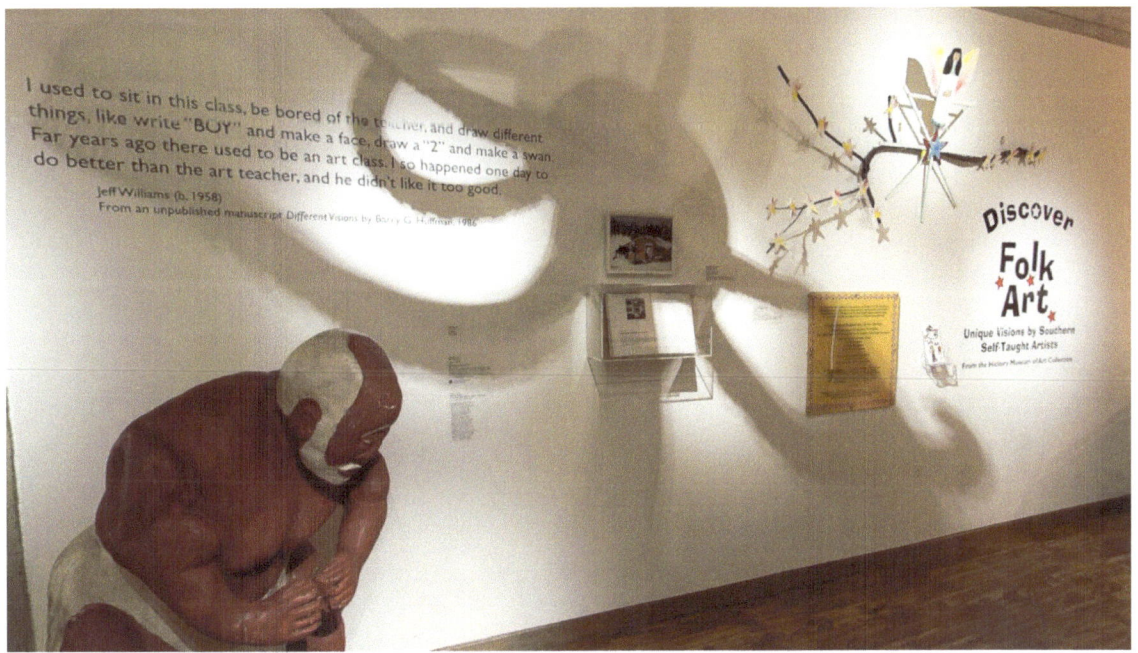

Hickory Museum of Art installation of Sumo by Jeff Williams. Photo: Ardath Weaver

This material has been edited from taped interviews. [Brackets] are used to indicate words that have been inserted for clarity. While not always 'the King's English,' regional speech is often lovely and personal. It imparts a sense of place and culture.

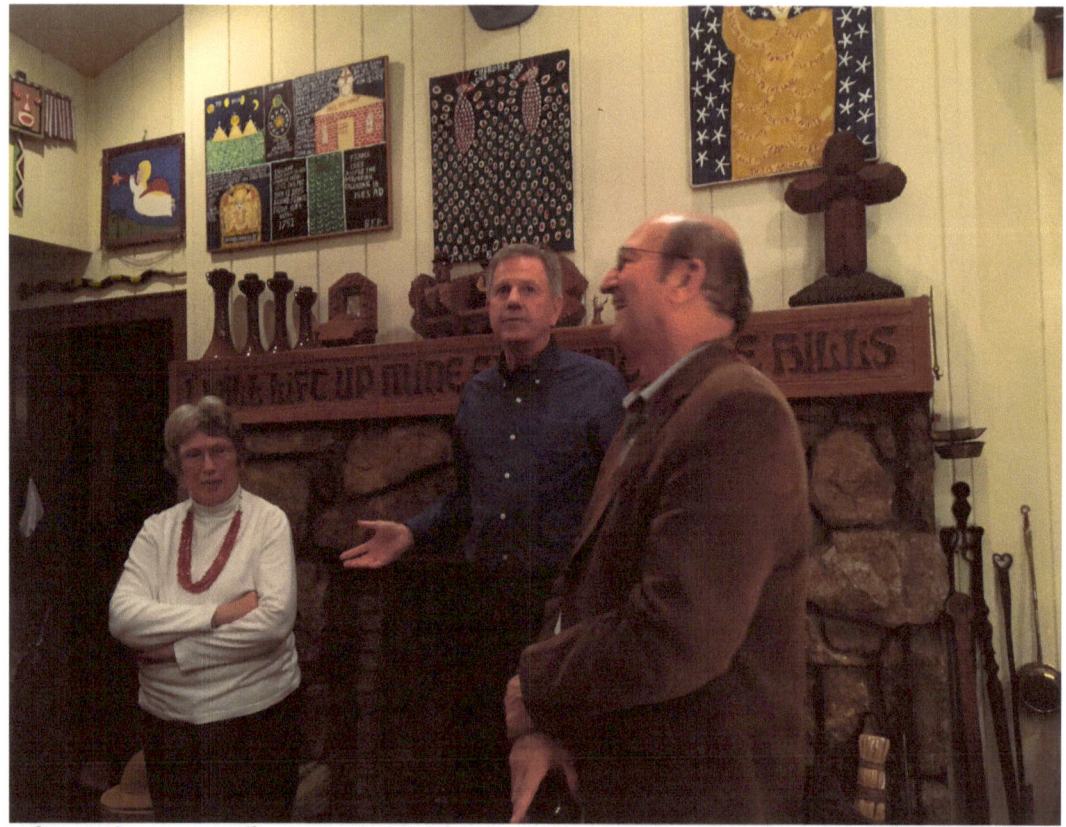

Left to Right: Barry Huffman, North Carolina Arts Council Director Wayne Martin, Allen Huffman in the Huffman's home in 2014.

ABOUT THE AUTHOR

Barry Gurley Huffman is a North Carolina native who has lived in Hickory for several decades. A noted collector with her husband Allen, she is the author of *Catawba Clay: Contemporary Southern Face Jug Makers* (1998) and *LaFone Living Art* (2015). A self-taught artist, she is currently working on a series of paintings of small churches in western North Carolina.

INTRODUCTION

This book is an invitation for you to meet a group of remarkable artists. You might be surprised to discover these regionally and often nationally recognized artists living quietly in rural North Carolina. They could easily pass for your grandparents or cousins or neighbors. Indeed, they may be. But there is something unique and wonderful about each of them — a creative drive that compels them to produce vital art. They work in a diversity of media, but they are drawn together by some common threads. Most are natives of the communities in which they live.

Except for Burlon Craig, who learned his craft from his neighbors, they have taught themselves a skill, then applied their personal vision to render some astonishing art. This work is perhaps unexpected, but it adds a rich cultural texture to their lives and to ours. While isolation may have been a shaping factor in part of their lives, they live in an age of modern communications. Their experiences with the 'public' world provide their art with more stimulation than contamination.

It is fashionable to term the work of self-taught artists 'Folk Art.' There are almost as many definitions of folk art as there are artists but perhaps it will suffice to tell you what they call themselves — a picture painter, a wood carver, a potter, a rock worker. Some think of themselves as artists, others do not. But their work demonstrates a certain directness of expression that has been evident in man's art since the early cave dwellers. The simplest lines define form, and embellishment of that form may be primitive in feeling. The statements made by their work are truths that transcend the barriers of culture and language, of age and experience, to touch people who care about individual visual expression.

Art has never been essential to mankind's survival. Only in recent centuries has it been possible to put food on the table by engaging solely in creative production. Certainly, it can be said that art greatly enhances the quality of life and brings pleasure to those who create it and to those who appreciate it.

Our artists provided for themselves and their families in traditional ways, but when time allowed, they filled spare moments with artistic endeavors. In their later years when other tasks became too difficult, they turned to their 'hobby,' their passion. For them, to create became a basic need. The acquaintance of these extraordinary people has been an extraordinary pleasure. They face the circumstances of their lives without pretense or self-importance. Their view of life is straight forward yet engaging, and their work reflects that sense of honesty. They have given us the gifts of their visions. And they have given graciously, because individually they are fine people. It has been a privilege and a joy to know them and to share them with you.

Minnie Smith Reinhardt (1898-1986) painted familiar scenes of rural Catawba County. Her memory paintings illustrate daily farming activities specific to each season, documenting the work of country living at the turn of the twentieth century in exquisite detail.

I was jus' real interested in it. If you're not, you don't want to mess with it. You can't do nothin' without bein' interested an' wantin' to do it more than anything else — that's the main thing.

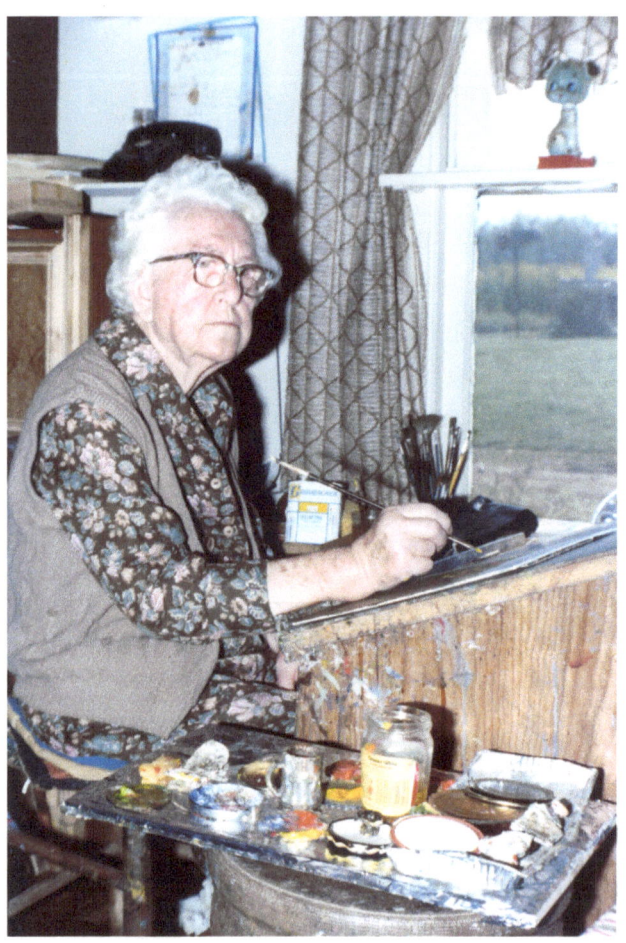

Interviewed in Vale, NC: January 10, February 22, April 26, and May 15, 1983

Minnie Reinhardt

MINNIE REINHARDT – ARTIST

January first, 1898, New Year Day, I was born. Born here, here where I live. Our ol' home burned up years ago, where I was raised. Right below here. I was born an' raised right here. There was eleven of us in the family. One died about six weeks old, and one was about twelve year old. She had appendicitis, an' back then they didn't operate. She died before I was born.

[Mother was a] Fulbright. The Fulbright's an' the Wyant's owned all this land through her — they owned thousands of acres through here. My Daddy made ware[1], an' he farmed, an' he hauled ware in his covered wagon. He'd haul it off an' maybe take a load to the mountains an' trade it for cabbage an' apples, irish potatoes. Sometimes he'd take a load to Charlotte — down there. He kept horses, maybe sometime have a half-a-dozen. It took alot to feed 'em — we raised the feed on the farm. My Daddy stayed on the road a lot.

I picked cotton, bound wheat, an' anything there's to do in the field. Mostly the money crop was cotton — raised the wheat to eat. My Daddy would cut wheat; he was the main one a cuttin' the wheat. That's worse than pickin' cotton — bindin' wheat. They didn't raise any cotton anymore through here.

I guess about seven year old, we walked about 3 mile to Hog Hill[2], across that foot-log[3] on the creek. Sometimes it'd be froze over an' we'd fall in. There was about half-a-dozen of us. We'd carry a basket of food — a big round home-made basket. The whole family'd eat in that. We didn't each one carry their lunch. Had sweet potatoes, fried pies [from] dried apples, maybe a little sausage. We'd butcher hogs in the winter. It was about all one could do to carry that big basket.

We'd start I reckon along about September — about 6 months, sometimes not that much, schoolin' in a year. And it'd be so cold — seemed like it was colder back then, an' snowy. We didn't go too much. About all I wanted to do when I went was t' set a drawin' a picture. I didn't learn much in a book. Some of 'em would bring crayons. There was holly trees on the creek. I could make holly an' red berries. We had slates; I could draw on them snow pictures — made pretty snow pictures on a slate [with] chalk — that was all I was interested in — of course after I got older, I forgot about it.

When I was about ten year old, typhoid fever come on me. [Dr. Fred T. Foard] was my doctor. He gave me some kind of a big ol' pill — it taste like a mad wasp smells — you know how they smell — that's the way it tasted. He'd come ever' day. He was a faithful doctor. He'd take in children that was left or didn't have anything, an' send 'em to school. He was good-hearted.

---

1 Wade Smith, Mrs. Reinhardt's father, was one of several farmer-potters in the area. He made alkaline glazed stoneware utilitarian pieces, such as jars, jugs, churns, and milk crocks.

2 Hog Hill School

3 Foot bridge made from a log

When I was a growin' up — pretty small — Zeb Ritchie was the closest [potter] to us. He was almost in sight back here. Zeb an' Munroe (Munroe was his Daddy), Munroe was crippled-like. He was in that ol' Confederate War. They made ware — there's a lot through here that did. Now Jim Lynn turned[4] a lot for my Daddy. [Jim] didn't have no shop 'til later. He was over there close to where Burl runs[5]. Jim turned a lot for my Daddy. Jay Propst and his son Sam, they turned and made — lived right up above Zeb's. But Wade Johnson was the main one. They call that Jugtown[6], I reckon 'cause the little post office was there. I don't know where they learned it, they just did it. All through here.

My brother turned a lot. My brother, Robert, the oldest one, he was twenty some year older than me. He got killed. I can remember helpin' some carryin' it out. Your feet'd nearly burn up a carryin' it out a that kiln.[7] You'd have to get down in there. We was small, we could walk up nearly straight. We'd have to carry it out, my brother (I had a brother younger than me) and me. [Dad'd] load it on a covered wagon an' take it to the mountains or either down to Charlotte, sometimes go to South Carolina. He'd trade it out mostly. Back then there wasn't much money.

When I was about eighteen I worked at Lenoir Rhyne College[8]. Some of my neighbors (girls) worked there, an' they wanted me to go with 'em, an' I went. I learned a lot there. Them girls[9] there was better to me than they was to each other. They'd get me up in a room an' play checkers. There was an ol' lady teacher, a homemaker teacher, Miss Morrell from New York, an' she'd let me go in there an' sew. I made my own clothes. There's where I learned to sew an' not use a pattern. Then I sewed for the public after I was married. I measured an' cut my own patterns. I never bought a pattern. They'd bring me a picture of what they wanted, an' I'd cut out a pattern an' make it. I sewed for the whole country — they'd come from Lincolnton an' Hickory.

I made ever one (of my children's clothes), an' a lot of 'em I made out of sacks. You'd get feed[10] sacks, an' you'd get this coarse white [sack and] dye it a pale color. Starch it a little. That was pretty, it looked like linen. And then there was feed sacks that was flowered pretty, that they made. Along when Hoover[11] was in, people'd just about perish. That was bad. Belton worked ten hours at the sawmill for a dollar a day — ten cent an hour. Glad to get it.

[Belton and I got married] about nineteen an' twenty one. He was back awhile.[12] [We had]five

---

4 To make pottery
5 Where Burlon B. Craig has a pottery
6 Named for post office location, name used by area residents (Wade Johnson's home and shop)
7 Catawba Valley potters used a ground hog kiln about 3 feet tall in the interior
8 A Lutheran College located in Hickory
9 The students
10 Cloth sacks containing cattle feed
11 President Herbert Hoover during the depression
12 From World War I. Belton served in France.

Minnie Reinhardt

girls an' one boy. It takes a lot for that many. We stayed here with my Dad an' Mother 'til they died. Took care of 'em. My Mother was still a livin' when the old house burned. That was a big ol' two story log [house]. That was the awfulest fire. It burned down about [nineteen] thirty.

I had my eyes operated on for cataracts. I was almost blind. I couldn't tell green from blue. After that [operation] everything looked so pretty an' bright. I told my daughter Arie I believed I'd go to paintin' pictures. So Christmas she brought me some paints, an' I set down an' started on it. I didn't know nothin' about paint. I never had any. I had to get me a book an' kinda learn how to mix it. I was about seventy-seven — along there.

My first picture was a little ol' log cabin with a lake sittin' behind it. That's what come on my mind. It jus' come to me. I don't know how —couldn't hardly tell you. Like the cotton fields an' wheat fields that I worked in, makin' molasses, neighbors, the church, Doc Foard's house. I was jus' real interested in it. If you're not, you don't want to mess with it. You can't do nothin' without bein' interested an' wantin' to do it more than anything else — that's the main thing. First, I check[13] my board off in about 4 blocks each way — that way you can put things more even in the right place. Then mostly I sketch off a house, maybe sometimes a barn. I jus' paint it on with a brush. Then the sky. [For] the ground I use burnt or raw amber, then put your light on there like sun hittin' places. Go back over it several times. About all of 'em has a house. I think they look more alive. I like to put people an' live things, dogs, in it. I like dogs an' live things.

I din't know one color. I didn't know burnt or raw umber or nothin' like that was. I got this book an' it told an' showed how to mix it, an' make different colors. And the color I jus' used my own imagination like for the sky, an' what I thought looked right.

Arie an' Virgil[14] was goin' — it's been a year ago —over there to [an art teacher]. They went to this woman. I don't know who she was. She told — I reckon I'm goin' to be a smart-aleck — Arie that if I'd had trainin' I'd a went a long ways. And I said "Well how come she didn't go a long ways?" She had trainin' an' was a teachin' art. How come she never won a prize? She had 'em in the bank.[15] She never won a prize. I said "Ask her that!" I don't know if they did or not, but that kinda made me mad. I'm jus' a doin' what I want to do. She had Arie to paint a sky an' put green in it. Well, that didn't look like the sky. An' Arie didn't like it. She didn't put it in it. They quit goin', and I don't know what they went for anyhow. They could paint good, both of 'em. It ain't a bit of use to go to an art teacher.

If you don't know, you're gonna paint the way you want to anyhow — the way you see it. You

---

13 To rule off a grid pattern of squares
14 Arie Taylor, Mrs. Reinhardt's daughter, and Virgil Smith, her nephew
15 First Union National Bank's annual Art Show in Hickory

don't want to do what somebody else [does]. Well, they[16] don't know too much. Most of 'em don't. I never did take an art lesson. I don't know what it is. I don't know what they'd do if you went, how they'd show you. Robby[17] was a natural artist, but he quit. He quit, Lord, he ain't painted nothin' in a year I reckon. You can't push 'em into it. But I enjoyed him a sittin' there with me, we was a paintin! Ohhh, he could sketch good. He could sketch it exactly like it. An' I mean in a couple of minutes, fast. He's about fifteen year old. He really had talent. He went to the art teacher up there at school. He said, "She won't never talk to me or nothin'." I said "You know the reason? You know more than she does!" He did. She couldn't tell him nothin.' I said, "Don't feel bad. You know more than her!" I hope he goes back.

I can remember how a lot of that ol' stuff [looked]. Our ol' homeplace, Doc Foards's place, Hog Hill, 'Possum John Rudisill, all of that. That picture I painted of 'Possum John in one room. Went in there a lot of times comin' from school. He hunted 'possums all the time in the winter, an' in the summer he'd fish.

I made[18] my ol' home places with an ol' covered wagon. I made it way back when I first started. We was a goin' to preachin'! We had to ride in the covered wagon a goin' to church ever time in the summer. My Daddy made us get in there, wouldn't let us walk. We'd rather walk an' have a little fun. He'd make us get in that ol' covered wagon back in there.

I can remember the first automobile. I was nearly grown. I saw my first automobile an' got rid in it. It felt like flyin.' It went off so easy. I was use to ridin' in an ol' wagon an' bouncin' over rock. Airplanes. We'd hear an airplane an' get out an' run, try to look where it was at. There wasn't no airplanes, I don't think, when he[19] was in that World War I. Maybe a couple.

I like them snow pictures. That's easier than[20] others. Like if you put in trees, you use right smart a shadow. I use a lot of Paynes gray in the sky too. I'm gonna start on 'em in a week or two. [People] like snow. There's an ol' lady lived down at Belmont. [She] come here an' bought snow pictures. She'd get her Social Security, an' here she'd come. She bought I don't know how many. Ever' one was a snow picture. Poor ol' thing. She was here last winter. Her husband stayed out in the car. She said, "I can't buy no more. He's got his legs cut off!" I didn't know what's wrong with him. I aimed to go out an' talk to him. They had the granddaughter — she's retarded an' they always bring her. I give her a little picture one time, an' it jus' tickled her so good. She was sittin' out there. It jus' made me sick that I didn't get to go out there an' talk to

---

16 Art teachers
17 Robby Sullivan, Mrs. Reinhardt's great grandson
18 Painted
19 Belton
20 To paint

Minnie Reinhardt

her, but them other people was here, an' got me sorta confused. My mind ain't too good no how.

There's a woman called me I bet it been a month ago. She said that she went to the same doctor (Dr. Gaither),that I went to. Said she saw a picture[21] wanted to know if it was for sale. I told her I had some here for sale. Well, she said she'd talk it over with her husband. Wanted to know how I sold 'em. I said "Here at home — a hundred dollars." She talked it over with her husband. I forgot about it. A week ago she started callin', from Hillsborough. Wanted me to tell her how to get here. I don't even 'call what direction [Hillsborough] was. I said "You'll have to go to Dr. Gaither!" He's the one that got her set in. "You go up there." Well, I reckon she called him up there. They gave her Sis.[22] She always takes me and she'll talk to them women in there.[23]

I guess they gave Sis's number. Wanted me to tell 'em how to get here. Well I didn't know how to tell her to get here. She finally got here after the awfulest callin' — long distance. After she got here, she's a school teacher. She had her mother with her. I thought she never a goin' to pick one out. She got the snow picture with an ol' house. She looked at that 'un, an' she looked at that 'un a haulin' the hay. The old lady — she was a fancy lookin' old lady — she said if she [wasn't] retired an' was makin' money, she'd buy that girl 'un for her birthday. Well, you know she had money. A lot of people got a lot of money, but they're gonna keep it. It ain't worth a nickel to 'em if they don't spend it an' get what they want.

I keep at [painting] about all the time. Not quite as much as I used to when I first started. But I don't never get tired of it. [I'll paint] as long as I can hold a brush in my hand. Like to do it as good as the day I started. Now I know a little more what I'm doing [than] when I first started. I don't want to sell too many, 'cause Lord, my pictures'll get gone. Just so I get enough [money] to run me, I don't care. I ain't goin' to be here long no how. Money wouldn't do me no good.

[My family] brought me at Christmas brushes an' paint all colors, a box full. I'll never need another bit. It's high— that paint an' brushes. A little ol' brush won't last long. But it come in good — that money — 'cause I spend a lot for medicine. People's been awful good to me. I'm grateful.

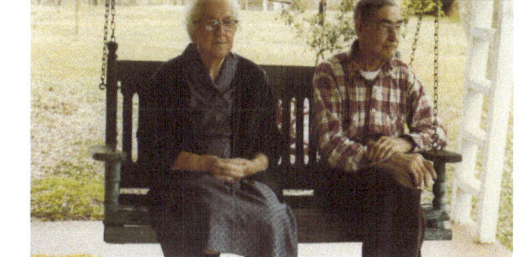

Minnie and Belton Reinhardt

---

21 In Dr. Gaither's office
22 Mrs. Reinhardt's daughter Sis (Dorothy Martin)
23 Dr. Gaither's office

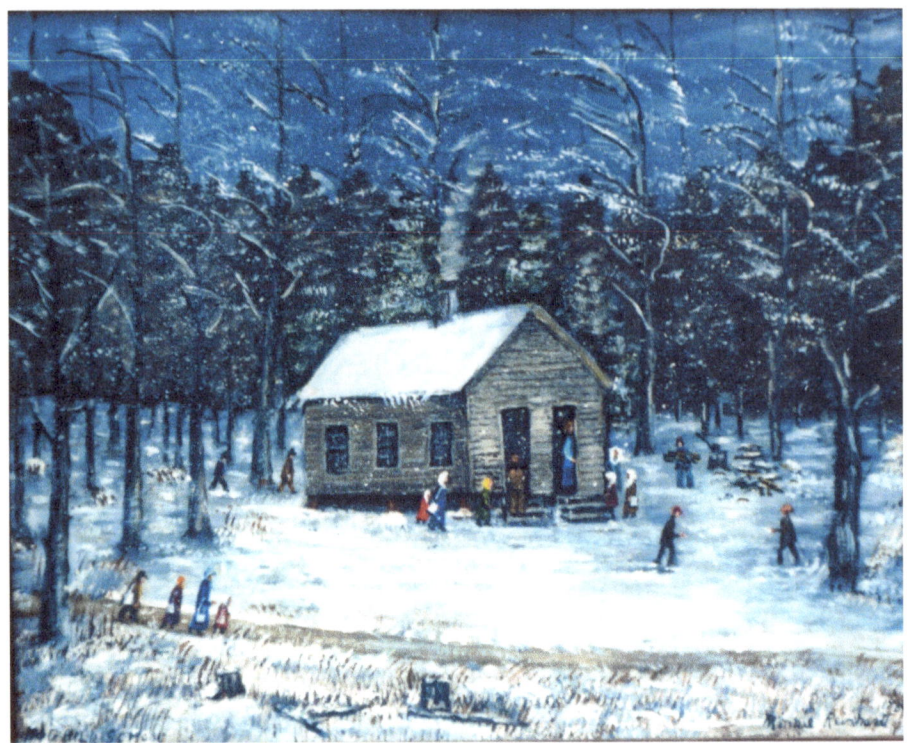

Hog Hill School

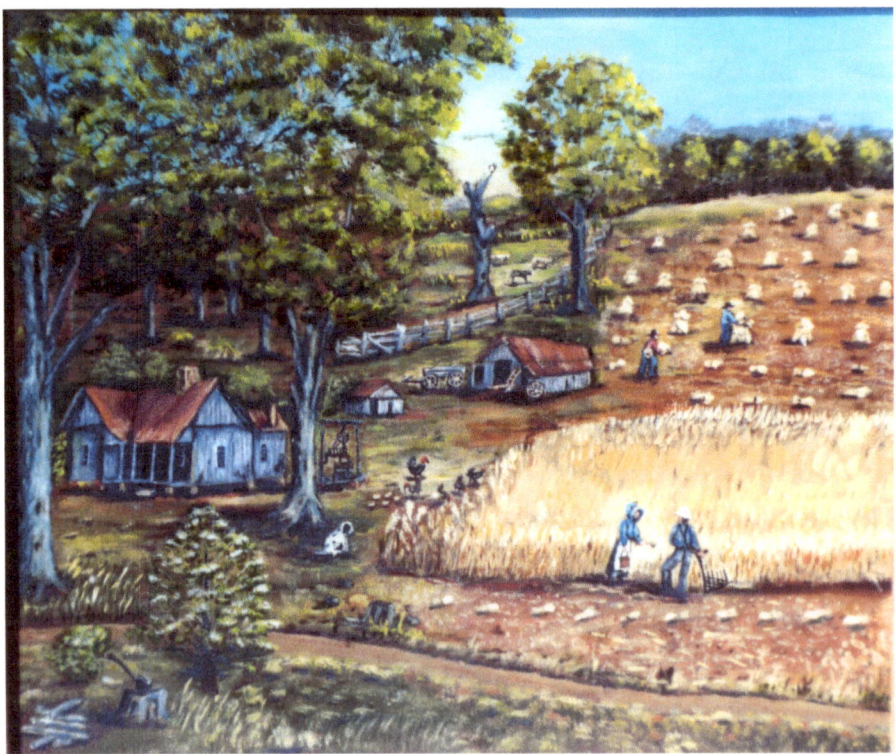

Cutting Wheat

Minnie Reinhardt

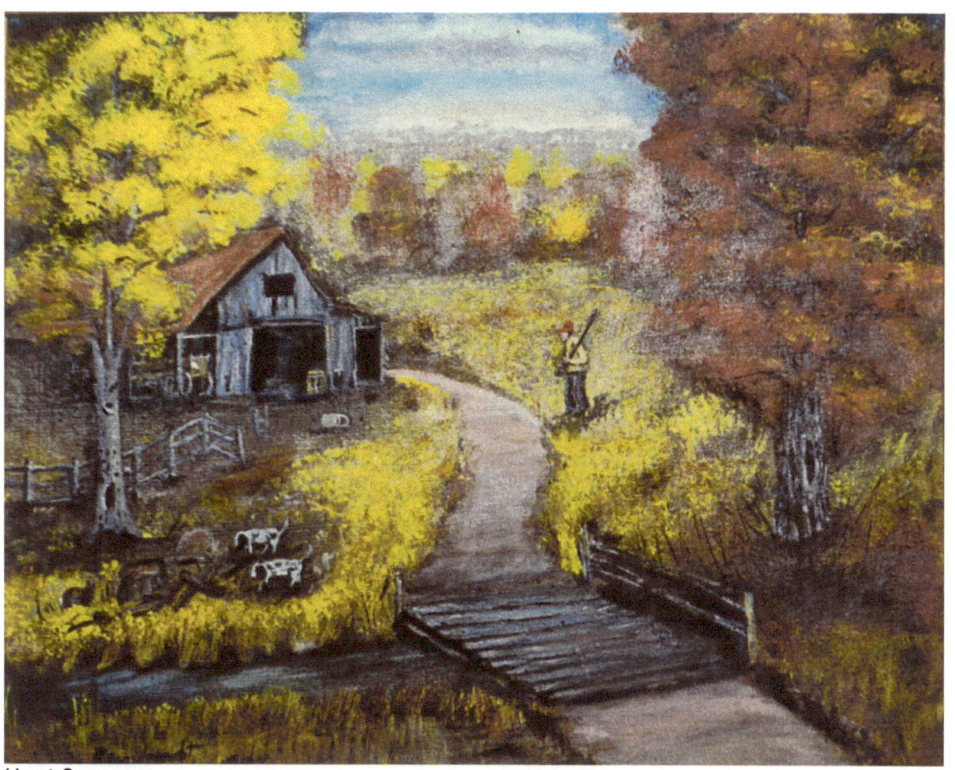

Hunt Scene

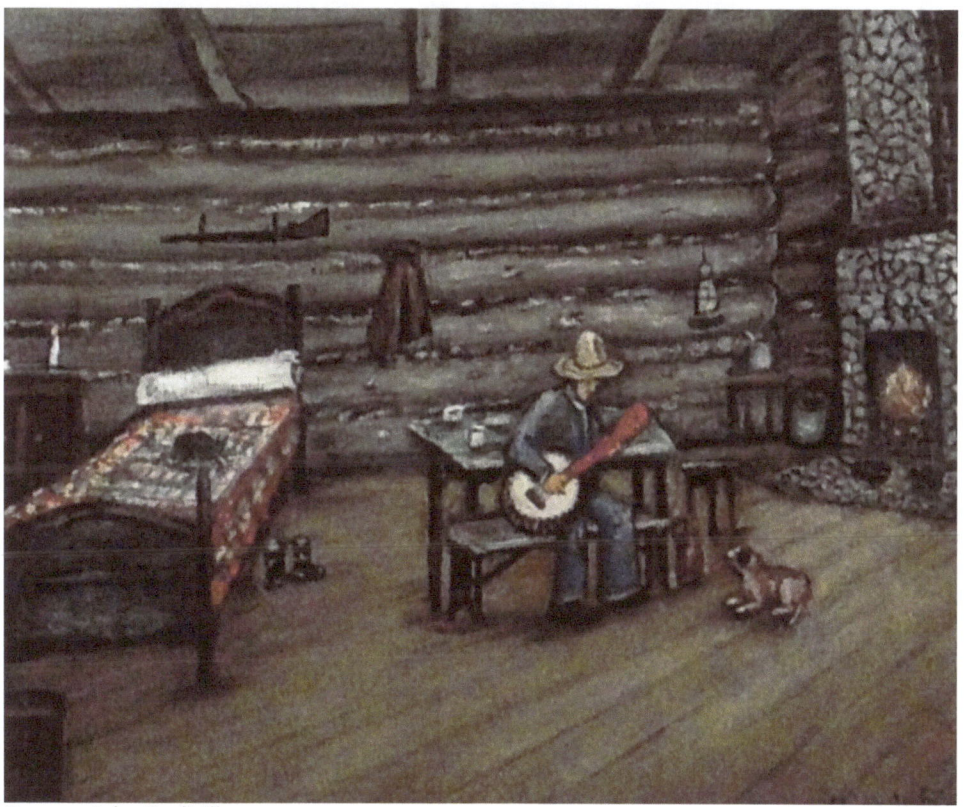

Possum John Rudisill

Raymond Coins (1904 - 1998) began woodcarving after retiring from farming at age 64, shaping the cedar and soapstone found around his home in the Westfield community near Pilot Mountain. He is known for carvings depicting dreams and biblical themes. He received the North Carolina Heritage Award in 1995.

I check the rock, an' pick out what I want out of it. I can jus' about see the picture in there.

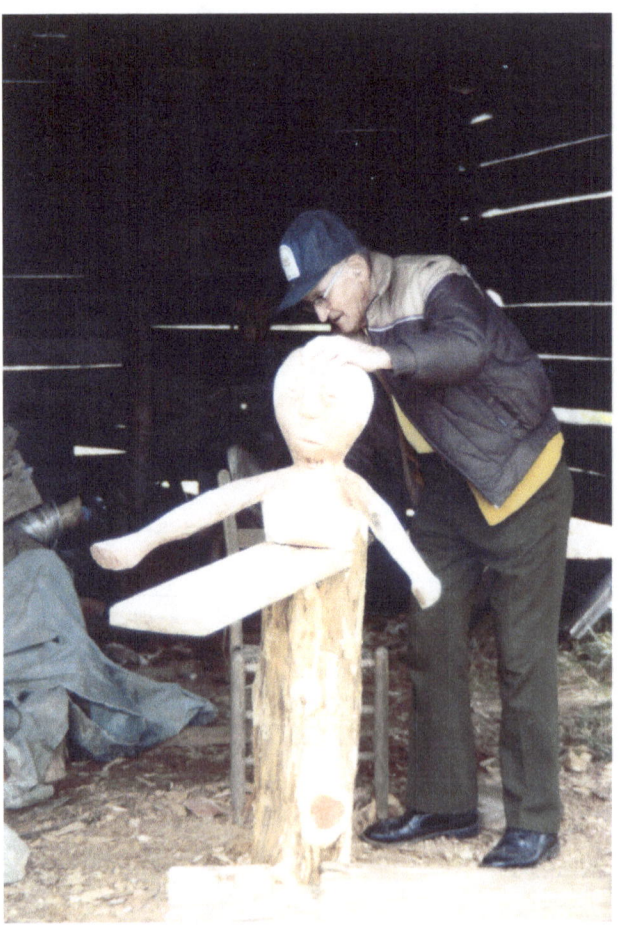

Interviewed in Pilot Mountain, NC: January 15, February 28, and March 6, 1983
Interviewed in Hickory, NC: December 19, 1986

Raymond Coins

Raymond Coins - Rock and Wood Worker

I was born near Stuart in Patrick County, Virginia, in 1904. All my folks [were from] Stuart an' Smithtown, Virginia. I never did find the place where I was born. The house burnt, they tell me. My Daddy moved to North Carolina when I was in the second year of school. I went to school here at Brims Grove. A preacher's house is built by the church there now. The second year I went to school, the teacher marched us out to the church to a grave. It was a baby to be buried. Some of 'ern told me that an' later that the baby was the first one to be buried there, an' I guess there's four hundred buried there now. Maybe more than that.

My Daddy rented land. [He] raised 'bacca[1], corn, wheat. He was jus' a farmer, an' never did gain nothin'. Jus' what we all eat. In the wind up you're jus' as well off.

Before I was old enough to go to school, an' I can remember when young 'uns wore dresses, they let my hair grow out. I can remember my Momma combin' my hair, an' it jus' killed me. I had a little box. I collected ever' thing you could think of, anything that was odd. I had that box plum full. When we moved to North Carolina, some reason, some how that box jus' got gone.

I didn't have much schoolin'. That's what hurt me. I've had to get by all these years, with, I reckon, [to] the fifth grade. We walked 3 or 4 miles to school. I wouldn't go at all unless they made me. They didn't have no law then. I'd rather work. I had a buddy [at school]. We had desks together. He was sharp an' he didn't have to study. We'd go to the blackboard to write spellin'. Well, I don't reckon I ever spelled or worked arithmetic that he didn't show me. He'd put [the answers] on a book an' hold it close where I could see it. I got by an' I didn't know nothin.'

So I've still lived without much education. Done a lot of hard work though, an' I might'd had a whole lot of education, an' I might a went to the pen.[2] After I quit school, an' got up big enough to run around a little bit, I had several buddies. A fella up the creek here, me an' him was real buddies. When they built the new school down here, one of 'em[3] put out for me to come to school. I didn't get no books. I went a year or two. I kinda had a big time. I didn't carry no books, but I'd go through the lessons. As much as two sat at a desk then. We'd all the time pick at one another. Ever' time we'd get a chance, we'd stick a pin in our shoe, an' stick one another with it. But all of 'em, they didn't laugh at me about the lesson, 'cause they knowed I didn't know the lesson no way.

---

1 Tobacco
2 Penitentiary
3 One of his buddies

Now I've been on top of Pilot Mountain.[4] They won't let you go up on top of it anymore. I was about 15 year old — a boy [from] over at Pinnacle[5] an' me went up it. He'd been up it. He told me to jus' follow him an' not look back 'till we got to the top. Some places you had to go up on the rock on the side of the mountain, an' then climb up on a wooden ladder. So he went in front an' I jus' followed him on. We got up there an' I set down. I'd a give ever' thing I would have owned if I'd been back to the bottom. We stayed up there about an hour. I'm sorta peculiar about gettin' up high. A pegged-leg man came up there, an' that helped me a whole lot. When I got older, I stayed with a man an' his wife for two or three year, right close to home, on account of there being so many at home.[6] I worked for them.

I got baldheaded when I was about 17 years old. It was the [most] embarrassing thing I ever knowed. I'd wear out ever' hat I'd get a hold of. When I started out a courtin' around, an' they'd call me "Baldy", it'd jus' kill me.

[I married Ruby King in December, 1926.] Her Daddy sold us a big house and 30 acres of land. I oughten never tore [that house] down. There weren't two in this country like it. It was sound as a dollar. All it needed was a top on it. He sold us that house for $500. There was a basement with two fireplaces downstairs, an' two fireplaces upstairs. All of it was hewed with a broad axe. It was put together pegged. Ever' door an' window had a peg in it. It was [built] back in slave time. I tore down a slave house an' built me a hog pen out of it, an' burnt the rest of it for wood.

I farmed an' worked in a warehouse.[7] I'd make a crop[8] an' then leave [the family] to tie[9] the 'bacca. I had twelve acres [in tobacco]. I used to have furnaces to heat the barns.[10] I'd have stacks of wood cut an' hauled in March. Now I worked. I'd get up ever' mornin' an' go feed the mules first thing, then milk the cows an' feed the hogs. Then Ruby'd have breakfast ready. You couldn't make somebody believe the way we worked. I worked all my life. [I raised] 'bacca, corn, an' wheat, rye, oats. I never did get started makin' no hay like some people. I always jus' bought my hay to feed my animals. We used to cut tops[11], cut corn, cull fodder, have corn shuckin'.

The whole neighborhood'd come in to help you shuck corn, fix a big dinner. We started havin' choppins[12] in January an' chop sometime through March. We'd get 15 or 20 hands to cut wood

---

4 The mountain from which the nearby town received its name
5 A nearby community
6 There were 13 children in the family.
7 Large warehouses where tobacco is sold seasonally
8 Of tobacco
9 Tie bunches of tobacco leaves to sticks to prepare for curing
10 Heated barns dried or cured the tobacco leaves
11 Out of tobacco
12 Cut wood to use to heat the tobacco barns

Raymond Coins

with an axe an' a cross cut saw. It was all day choppin' [with] dinner an' supper.

I guess I lost ever' year I worked in the warehouse. I'd work one year an' say, "Well, I'm not goin' to do this no more!" But everybody'd get after me, an' I was right back. So I worked in the warehouse an' I farmed too. That'd throw me to sell my 'bacca late — used to, way back yonder, 'bacca'd go down[13] some at the last of the market. I still don't think I gained anything by workin'. I was a floor man. It used to be my job to get out on the floor an' show 'em where to put the 'bacca. We'd put a ticket on it.

Harvey Lynch[14] learned me how to put on a sale. Of course I could read a little more so back then. I guess the warehouse work took me about 13 weeks [a year]. I could always get by with the warehouse work. If I hired, I'd tell 'em,[15] "Now, I'm gone to tell you one thing right now — I ain't gone to steal from nobody." They'd catch workers [warehouse] stealin' sometimes. I worked in the warehouse 25 or 30 years all together. [Tobacco] is about over with now. If anyone had told me that [tobacco] would come to an end, I wouldn't have believed it.

I joined Rock House Primitive Baptist Church in 1936. They appointed me deacon the first year I joined the church. At that time, all the Primitive Baptists were together, an' they were in correspondence from coast to coast. We had about 30 churches in the Fish River Association, an' it was in a correspondence with all the other associations. Then a bunch of 'em got to preachin' absolute predestination. They let 'em preach it until it come to a bust up. They divided up on absolute predestination — a bunch of them was preachin' that God Almighty absolutely predestined ever act of man, both good an' evil. If one taken a gun an' shoot ya, God predestinated him to do that. Then they kept dividin'. They divided I don't know how many times. The Missionary an' Primitive Baptists was together one time jus' like they was before the Absolute divided — but the Missionary Baptists was good enough to taken the name of Missionary, an' didn't try to take the name of Primitive Baptist.

But we stayed with the Rock House Church. I try to do the best I can, but we got a lot that jus' any way an' ever way an' we have had bad reports on 'em all over the whole country. Then they'll go to somebody an' say "We're Primitive Baptists!" Then ever one tryin' to stand an' live as a Baptist have to take the blame for the ones that don't know the difference. That's the way it stands.

I retired at 62 I thought, but when my age come back[16] I was 64. I got that old overnight. I was

13 In price
14 His neighbor
15 His employers
16 From social security

gonna retire an' sit down, do nothin'. I done that about a year. You get tired a doin' nothin.' That's the worse tired anybody can have. You can't live when you get tired of doin' nothin'.

I got started on the rock statues — how come me to get started on that? Harvey Lynch, my neighbor, me an' him always been buddies. Might nigh[17] all our lives, so I found a rock up [at his farm], that was cut out. I forget what shape. I sold it to an antique man[18] way back yonder. I found out rock would work. I started makin' tommy hawks an' Indian bowls. I'd split me a hickory stick an' put [the rock] on the stick, an' tie a leather string around it. Back at that time, I sold it for about five dollars. I sold one I know of, a fella kept it a year an' sold it for a hundred dollars.

Then I got to makin' little bitty dolls. I kept leadin' from one thing to another. And it was real good. I started makin' Indian dolls, an' I kept makin' 'em bigger an' bigger an' bigger 'till I made one that weighed 500 pounds. I made an alligator that took four [men] to load it. There was a great big rock layin' down there. A fella sent down there an' looked. I said "I want you to tell me what you want made outa that rock!" He looked at it an' said, "Can you make an alligator?" I said "Yeah, I can make an alligator." It taked four of 'em to put it in a pick-up. I guess it weighed 700 pounds. I made big stuff back yonder.

I got a rock saw, but I ain't got the right blade. I got a sander. I chisel the rock with a little ol' axe, I wore it out, about, it's got a broke handle. I can turn the rock up this way an' that way, an' see where to make [cuts], I've made bears. I've made some jus' real ol' bears. Set the rock up like that. Now one time I thought it would make a great big ol' chicken, an' finally wound up — I turned it around. I decided it'd make a bear. Made a bear, a bear's head is down anyway. I check the rock, an' pick out what I want out of it. I can jus' about see the picture in there. Then take the chisel an' axe, cut it down, then sand it.

I made several cats outa rock. Gordon's bank up here — that's been years ago — I dealt with him for years an' years. I carried cats in there, an' they went wild over 'ern in the bank. So I said, "Wick, I'm jus' gonna give 'em to you. I thought they'd set 'em up. I thought it was for advertisement. An' you know, he sold 'ern. I know the woman that bought 'em. What'd I'd sell you for ten dollars would cost him a hundred dollars to ever get another piece. [A man] bought [from me] about 3 years. I contracted with him not to sell to anybody else. He said if I'd promise that, he'd buy all the rock, an' we wouldn't fall out about the price. So we always got together some way, somehow on the price. Then he called me later an' said he'd take all the wood work.

---

17 Near
18 Antique dealer
Raymond Coins

Ol' lady Brennan carried a lot down somewhere to sell 'em. She'd come an' pick it up for a long time. She'd want to buy it on credit. She had plenty of money. Her Daddy owned that Pinnacle Mountain. She'd want to give me a paper "I Owe You." I got tired of it. I don't even care about her comin'.

It weren't too long after I started [workin' rock that I started the wood]. I went to the lake. My son-in-law had a trailer on the lake, an' I got some [wood]. I made a lot of small stuff outa wood — owls — stuff like that. But [at first] I used to make all big [wooden pieces]. I wouldn't even know how many I have made. I got a piece of wood one time an' made a deer — it was might nigh like a deer head an' long neck an' everything. I made a donkey one time. I don't even know hardly what I have made.

I pick out a tree with arms an' legs, an' limbs that stand up. If I see a tree with a fork to make legs an' the arms are up somewhere I can cut it all then cut a head on there. I really rather work on wood [than rock], there's not the dust. Cedar works pretty good.

I got interested in [the rock and the wood]. If I'm not interested, I don't care a'tal. If I go out to work an' I'm not interested, I stop. I ain't never been at this jus' a purpose for the money. I'm jus' interested in it. When I get a bunch made, I jus' love it. I've got rid of many of 'em when I get a bunch made. [They] sit here, an' I get attached to it some way. I've sold many a bunch, an' I've loved it too. But I don't put it ahead of nothin' else. If I want to go somewhere, then I go. If I had company, I ain't put it ahead of [visiting].

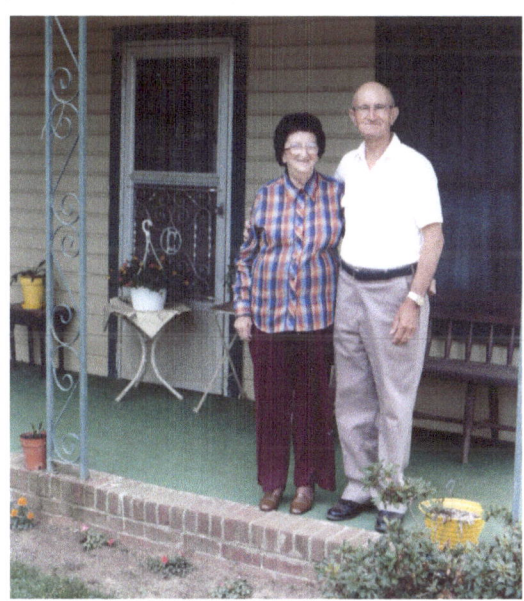

Raymond and Ruby Coins, July 1984

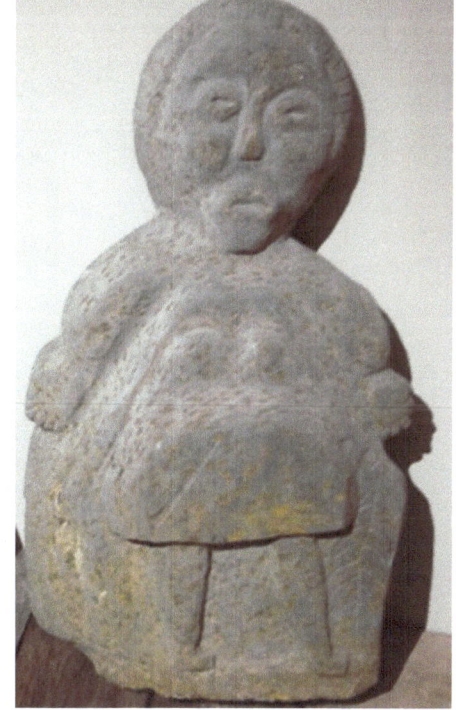

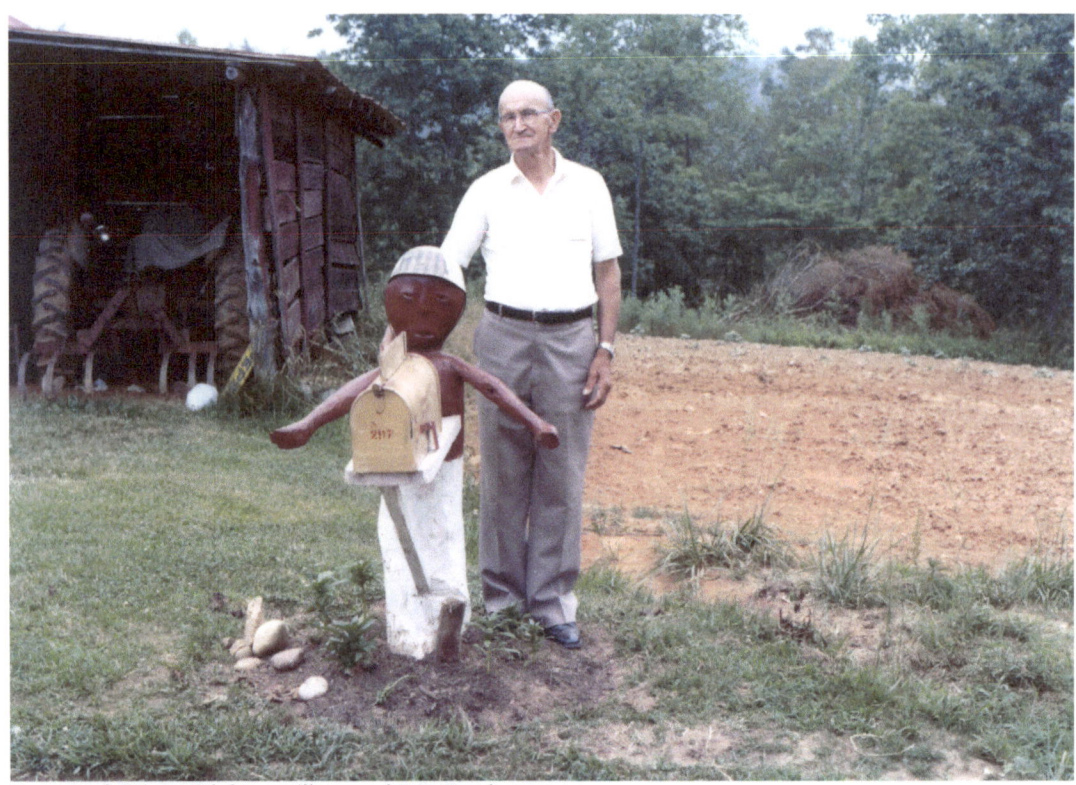

Raymond Coins with his mailbox and Dog Tombstone

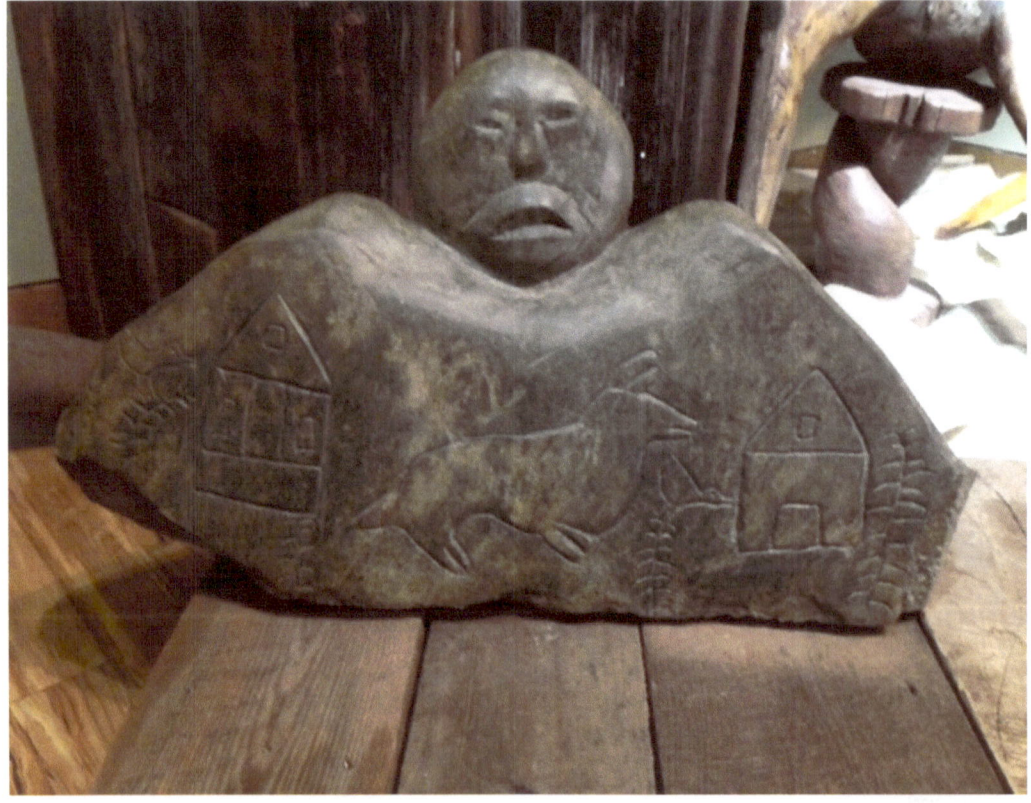

Raymond Coins

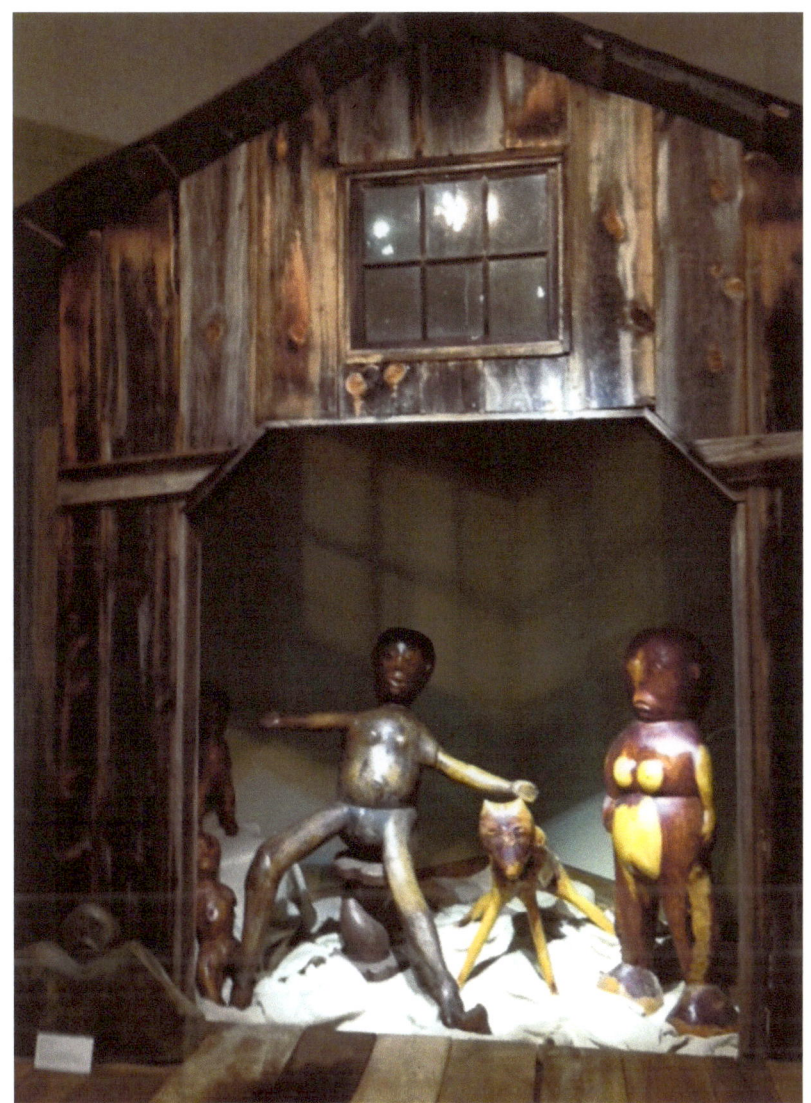

Hickory Museum of Art installation

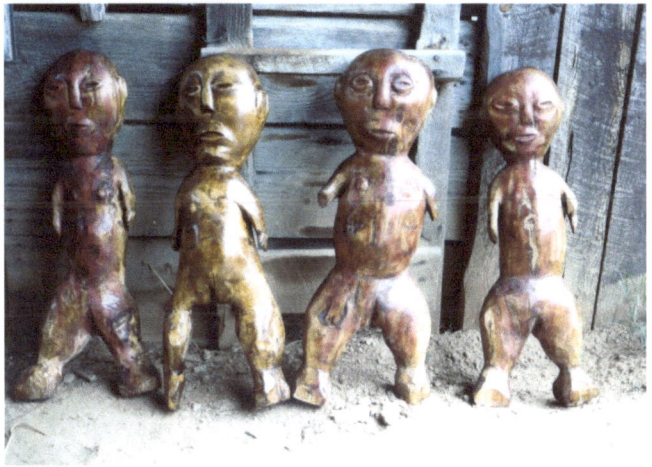

Baby Dolls

James Columbus Cook (1934 - 1984) is known for his carved and painted figures of people at work and play. Confined to a wheelchair after an accident, he credited his grandfather for his interest in carving.

A lot of [my] work reminds me of the past, and I use my imagination on most of my work. My imagination never ends on me.

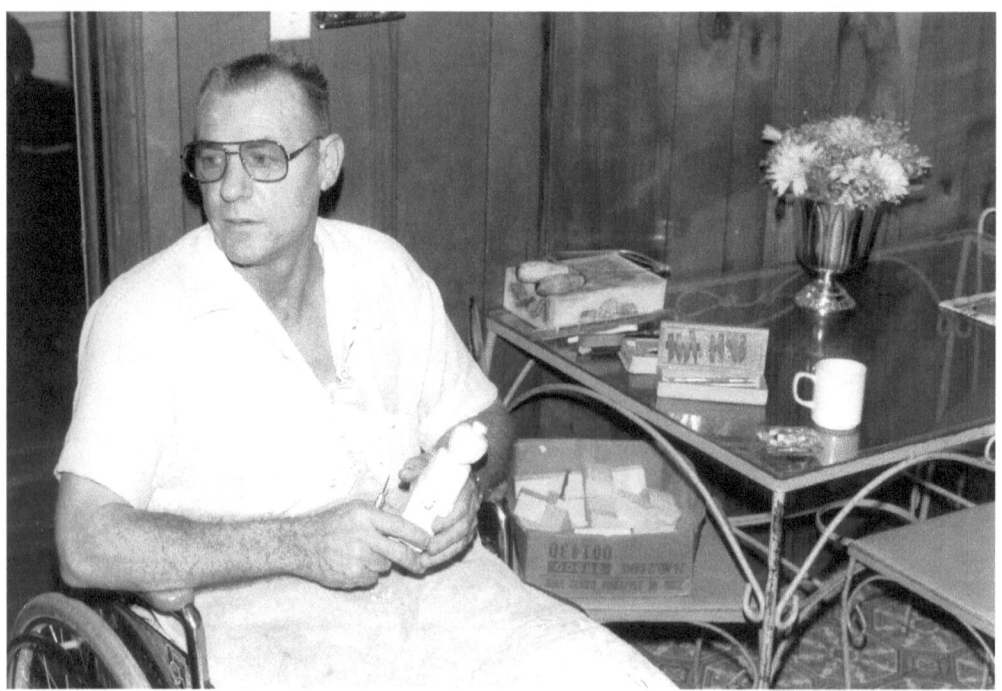

Interviewed in Lawndale, NC: January 17, 1984

James Cook

James Cook - Woodcarver

I was born 1934, second of September, at Glen Alpine in the mountains near Lake James. My parents is Reverend M. L. Cook, a Baptist minister, and my mother is Darless Poole Cook. They were from Cleveland and Lincoln County, and from one county to another. [We went] where [Dad] was preachin' and where he could rent a cotton farm and raise cotton.

On spare time I helped my grandfather. He was a carpenter. He'd build homes, cabinets, anything concernin' a home. That's how I got interested in woods, working with him. When I was eight/nine years old I made my own toys out of wood. I made wagons, toy guns, just about any type of toy that's on the market now in town. I used my father's tools, because on his spare time he would also help with carpentry. I'd use his tools of an evenin' and on the week ends. My grandfather was Columbus Cook from Lawndale.

I got married in 1953. I married Margie Lingerfelt, from Lawndale. I was in the Navy at the time, and after I got discharged, we settled down and built a home on Route 3, Lawndale. I have four children (one son and three daughters). They are married, and I have four grand children.

I had an accident after I was released from the Navy. I wasn't discharged, I was released. I broke my neck and [that] left me partially paralyzed from the waist down, which put me in a wheelchair. There's when I really got interested in the arts, because it was rehabilitatin' me and therapy, and also a real good hobby for me. So this kindly got me back on my wood work and art work.

I spent years on the lakes fishin' and tryin' things I shouldn't have, now I see, because I wasted all that time I should a been on my art work. I did my gardenin' and my yard work on a garden tractor, and I still do a little, but not like I used to. As far as fishin' and tryin' to get out and do sports like I did a few years back, I discontinued that. I don't try that no longer. I spend all my time carvin', and then time with my grandchildren and friends. Fishin' was my main fun and hobby and past time on the weekends and through the week. I miss the lake and the fast boats and the bass tournaments, but I'm gettin' over it now.

I started carvin' figurines professionally about 3 ½ years ago, but I carved figurines and did things related to figurines years ago something like twenty/twenty eight year ago. I did little animals, and carved birds, mallards, ducks, and things of that nature. I did that for friends, children, and my sisters and brothers-in-law, and people in the family. This gave me experience and knowledge on my folk art.

I use white pine, and that's all I use. A lot of woodcarvers use basswood, but I find I don't like to cut it. This white pine is a medium cut, and it holds up good, won't break so easy. I like the way it carves and sands and paints. [I do it] all by hand. I use all hand equipment; no power tools what so ever. I do my work like they would have done it a hundred years ago — all by hand. I take a block of white pine, and I'll draw my picture on it, and I'll take my coping saw, and saw the figurine out. I'll carve the figurine and sculpture it into the shape I want. Then I'll sand it and paint it. There's five steps to completion.

These furniture companies will have scrap wood they're going to throw away, and I'll get my scrap wood from them. The cost is very little. A lot of times I have to work around knots. I can't stand them suckers, but I find I can get a good end off a piece of wood.

I use X-Acto knives and blades. I have different types of blades I use. I try to slow up and make my painting a little better. I always see room for improvement. Sometimes it's hard for me to choose what colors I'll use, but I try to put the colors to relate to the man's job or whatever he's a doin', how he should be dressed for the situation.

I use acrylic water paint — best that I can buy. I haven't had any problems with it. It seems to do the job. Mostly, I put two coats [on it] on account of it makes it look a little thicker and better. If it don't bleed in so bad, then I can get by with one. Sometimes they'll get dirty and you can't wash it. You can repaint it and there's no problem. I'll do that as long as I live for free. If it gets broke, I also will repair it free.

A lot of [my]work reminds me of the past, and I use my imagination on most of my work. My imagination never ends on me. [I'm] a year ahead right now on imagination if I can put it to work. I'll be a carvin' one and I'll have another one in mind, and I can't wait to get to that one. Ever' time I do a new piece — like that hobo over there's one of the new ones I thought of this week. I did it yesterday. The reason for me to think of the hobo, I reckon, was because of a little scene I saw on T.V., and I thought it was cute. So I did it.

Now Uncle Sam there, it's an ol' commercial for the armed services, but a lot of imagination went into it. I can remember those posters when I was real young. They've changed him kindly, I think modernized his look a little bit. Whenever I do him on a piece of wood, I make him look the way I want him to. I don't go by posters.

My Indian — I do that Cherokee Indian because I try to go up to the Cherokee reservation in

James Cook

the mountains about twice a year. I pick up a lot of knowledge and information there. I visit a few museums and the Folk Art Center at Asheville. That area I love I reckon because I was born up near there.

The newsboy is a little different there. I like to do that to give the news media a little recognition. I like the Hickory Daily Record[1] and the paper they put out. I read it every day. They're really up on things. [Margie] gets it near our home at a service station where it's delivered each day.

Those little ladies, I always say a woman's job is never done, so I never run out of ideas. I do makin' bread, makin' quilts, and things related back to early years. I do the little ol' ladies a readin' the Bible. I can remember my grandma a sittin' readin' the Bible on Sunday afternoon. She always took time for the Bible. Over the years I feel like it's real good readin' material and a good habit. My father also followed the same trend. I do little ol' ladies makin' jelly and doin' just about anything you can find in a home that needs to be done. Margie gets a chuckle out of most of [the lady figurines] and says, "That looks like a true piece of work there, puts me in mind of me sometimes." Margie stays busy. She works in town eight to ten hours and puts in another five or six hours of a evenin' at home.

I do Father Frost, which is a Russian Santa, and I do the 1840 Santa with the tree, and I do the 1900's Santa with the bag of toys in it. And then I do the regular traditional Santa Claus. I do Santa on the sleigh with reindeers. I did my first nativity scene about three year ago, and it caught on pretty good. I did quite a few. And of course you can add on to those until you get what you want. I do anything concernin' Christmas holidays, occupations, hobbies and sports. I do it all.

In 1981 I was takin' work on a Saturday to the trade lot[2]. I'd do craft work, a little art work. Lynn Causby[3] — she came by and saw my work and kinda pushed me out of the closet with it. She called the Mint and told Stu Schwartz[4]. Stu came up here then. I had my work on that little table. When he opened the front door, he saw it. He didn't have too much to say to me, he just fell on his knees in front of it and said, "I want it all." I had twenty eight pieces there. There was somebody with him but he said, "I get all of those!" I looked at him. I thought, "Man, are you crazy? Wantin' all that shabby work?"

Museums keep me fairly busy. Quite a few museums write or call and ask me to send a sample piece of work, and a lot of times they'll call and say, "Send me some of your work," and they

---

1 A newspaper published in Hickory

2 Flea market

3 An artist from Morganton

4 Former curator of the Mint Museum of History in Charlotte

don't even see it until I send it to 'em. [Museums in] Delaware and California, and recently I sent some more work to Raleigh. And I sent some to the Folk Art Center at Asheville after Christmas. I sent them some for permanent display. About 95% of my work goes through the mail to various states. I have people who come to my home to get work, from Missouri, Florida, South Carolina, Charlotte, Hickory, Morganton, Lenoir, Shelby, just all around. I have some collectors that when they go on vacation they might be in the mountains, and I'm here in the foothills, so they take a day out and they come to see my work, and get some of it. It works out pretty good that way.

[The Folk Art Museum in New York] wanted watermelon men. They wanted all they can get. I told my wife "I'm going to do a black watermelon man and see how they like that." I did, and from four-five days later I got the watermelon man back, and a nice letter. I also got a phone call. They said they didn't want the black watermelon man — it was a stereotype. Some people workin' in the museum didn't like it 'cause it was a stereotype, so if I didn't mind, not to send 'em any more black watermelon men. I told my wife "They have the problem — I don't. All the black people I know like watermelon. They eat it just like the whites and other nationalities. I'm going to paint that thing, make a white man out of him and mail it back!" And I did and they had a fit over him. They didn't know the difference. So they sent my check then for the work. That's the only problem I ever had with New York. They said they didn't want any modern folk art. They'd rather have something relating back to farm work or something like that. They called before Christmas and ordered nine pieces of work. I didn't get time to do it. My collectors, I do them before I do the shops.

I put off two television [interviews] last year: one at Charlotte and one at Raleigh. I kindly avoid all that I can, 'cause I don't need it. I can't keep up with what I got now. I raised my prices, [but] they buy more. You see what happens. They say, "Well, I'm going to get me a collection before it goes even higher!"

In my family there's artists. All my father's people background worked with wood. My grandfather taught me a whole lot. My father was a carpenter, painter, lay brick and block, and general housebuilding. I did it all too. I draw up the plans for this house here when I had it built.

I can design, build, and do furniture. I can design furniture right now that would save 'em money on buildin' it, and would be more compact and practical for the home. I find a lot of these modern ways and methods, I don't like. Things is built now days for the money, quick turnover. They're not built to last no way.

James Cook

A man's experience and what he knows [is] what makes him the best, whether he's a lawyer or doctor or artist or whatever. You have to have the knowledge and education. Sunday I was talking to my brother-in-law [who] owns and runs this drugstore in Shelby. We all had a meeting over at my Dad's — they're gettin' old. My Dad's seventy-eight. He's still a goin'! For his age he's in pretty good health, but my mother's health's poorly now. We was talking about doctors — I said I was at the festival at Greensboro last year. This guy and two lovely children and beautiful wife — just wonderful, beautiful people — come to my table and looked at my work. He didn't have much to say to me. He wouldn't talk to me. He looked at my work and said, "That's real good work." He had his hair way down here in a ponytail tied up and beard down here. Tennis shoes with holes in 'em. And was dressed like some kind of a bum. And I said, "You know I don't usually say this about a man, but your beard — that looks good. You look good with that beard and long hair!" And he did. He honestly did. He flipped his card out and he was a surgeon! I just couldn't believe it. He cleaned my table off — bought ever thing I had. As I got his check I said, "Oh, yeah, that beard could use a trimmin' though." After I got his check. I thought my brother-in-law would crack up. He deals with doctors in the drugstore.

You gotta respect a man with education and kinda look up to him. I do. I didn't get a chance to get an [education]. I had a doctor recently say, "You'd make a good surgeon. You're real good with the detail work with a knife." I said, "Well, I'm still thinkin' about goin' into the brain surgeon business!" He just bent over laughin! He thought I was crazy.

The first reaction on people when they see my work, they say, "Law, I've never seen nothin' like this in all my life. That's the prettiest, best I've ever seen." That's the reaction on ninety percent. I don't know of ever havin' anybody go by my table[5] and not bein' kinda amazed at the work. They claim it's different and more realistic. Then a lot of 'em say "Is this ceramic?" I say, "No, it's all made out of white pine, all hand-carved." They say, "Did you do this?" I say, "No, my wife did." I have my fun with a lot of people. Then they start orderin'. Usually I sold out the early ones[6], then they leave it and come back to pick it up later. They'll leave it so I can show it. That helps.

[Carving] keeps me a goin'! I'm constantly busy. If I take time out, I get behind worse. I did a piece this morning already. I do anywhere from two to four a day. I can speed carve when I want to. Some days, if I feel real good and start early and work late, I can carve out four single pieces. They're yet to sand and paint. And of course accessories to go with it. But I can speed carve when I want to. If I was to enter some of these contests on speed carvin' which they have in Missouri or somewhere like that, I think I could win it. There's no doubt in my mind. But

5 Table at one of the craft festivals James attends
6 Early in the day

that takes you back to experience. I couldn't carve out the [four] pieces a day a year or so ago. Experience. You learn how to cut corners on it. You don't take a coffee break of anything like that. You stay with it if you carve out four a day.

A lot of work I do, I don't carve and finish it in a day. Just according to the details. Some of them I can do in a day. When I go to these festivals, people ask me, "How long does it take you to do a piece like that?" I usually say a day. I don't feel good enough to ever' day a speed carve. If I'd average it out, I'd have to say I do one a day and be honest about it. If I do one completed ever' day, it'd be more down to earth.

I usually get up somewhere around two, two-thirty in the mornin'. I got my alarms set for two-thirty. I'll get up and have my coffee and work a couple of hours, then have my breakfast. During the day if I need some circulation, stretch out or exercise a little, I'll go lay down for an hour or so, then go back at it. Usually about eight or eight-thirty of an evenin' I'll hang it up for the day. You get burned out kinda by then.

It's kinda run into a job now. The way I feel about it is I want to get all I can out there in people's homes. I'm not really worried about the museums. I can put 'em off, because I feel like they'll always be there. I'd rather have a piece in your home, really, truly, than at a museum because it's kindly a personal thing in somebody's home. Any museum can buy what they want. I like the collectors. The way I do, I get covered up in orders around Christmas time, holidays, and it kindly sometimes gets on my nerves. I work to get that out. But I back off then. If somebody orders, I say, "It may be two or three weeks. They say, "Well, I'm not in no hurry!" You can get pressure on any job I think.

It was a hobby, and it turned into a job. I enjoy it. I worked steady since about 1981. Since then I've had to do a piece at least ever' day. I mean holidays and all. When I'm goin' to a festival I'll cut out a piece there and do it. I'll work. If I go on a vacation or visit, I'll take a piece of wood and cut there.

I can't leave it alone.

James Cook

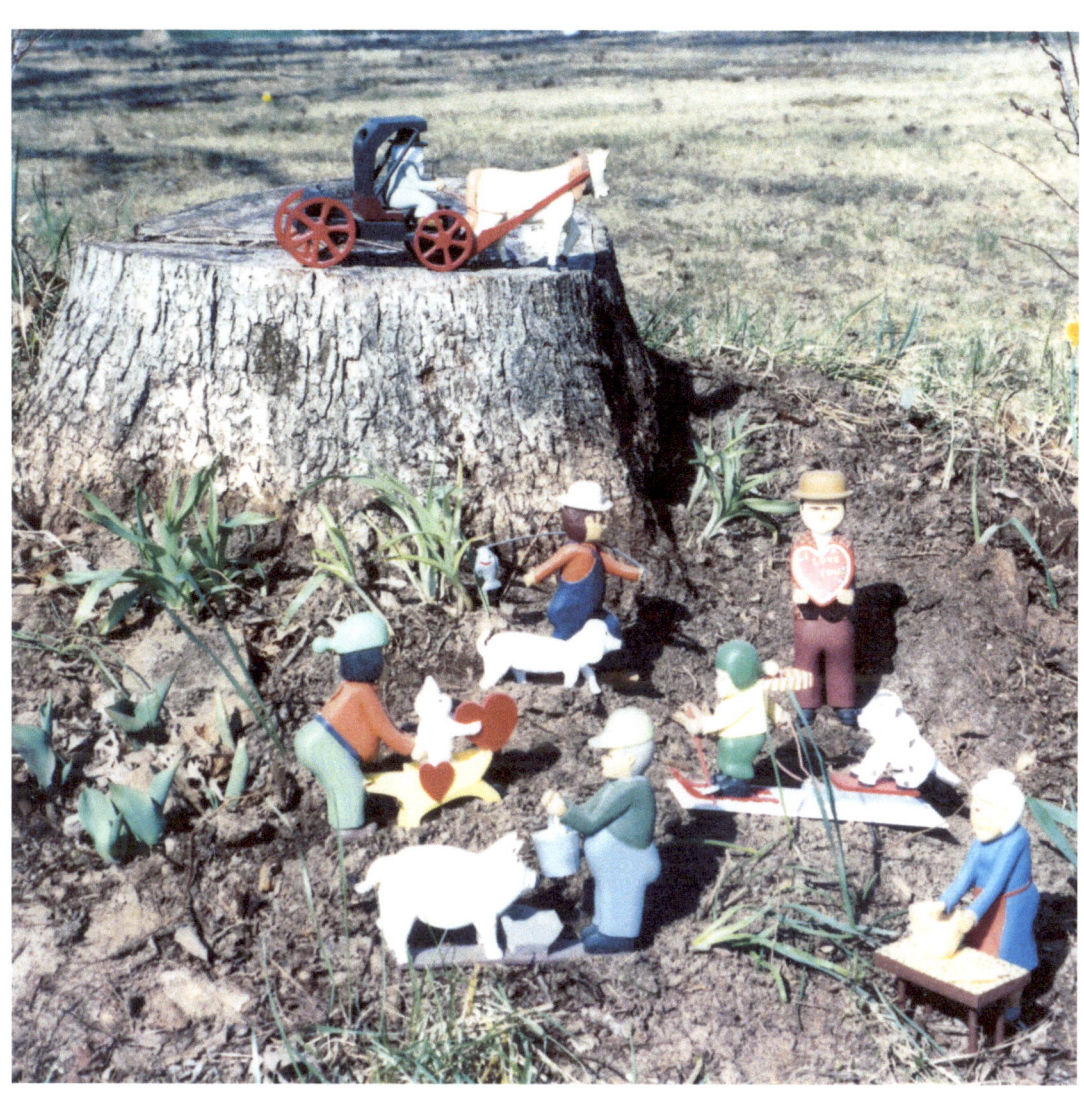

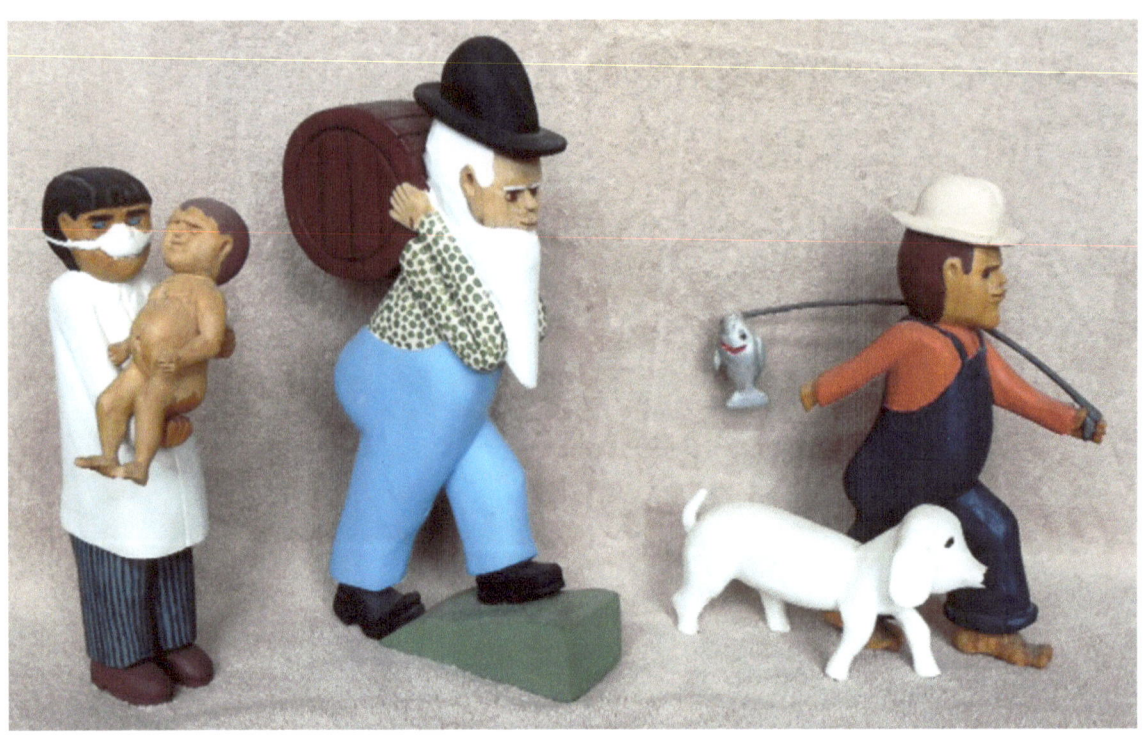

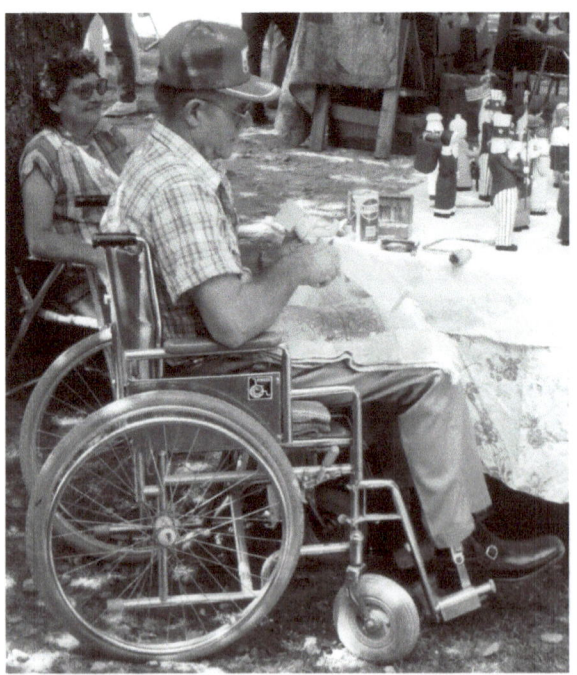

James and Margie Cook at Blowing Rock Craft Show

James Cook

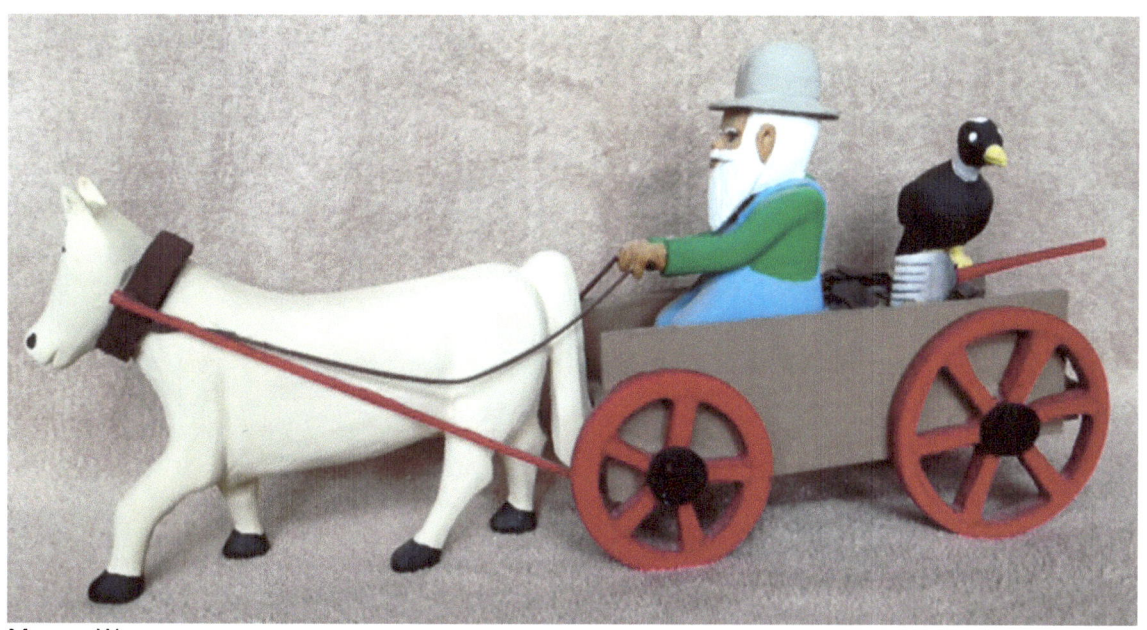

Manure Wagon

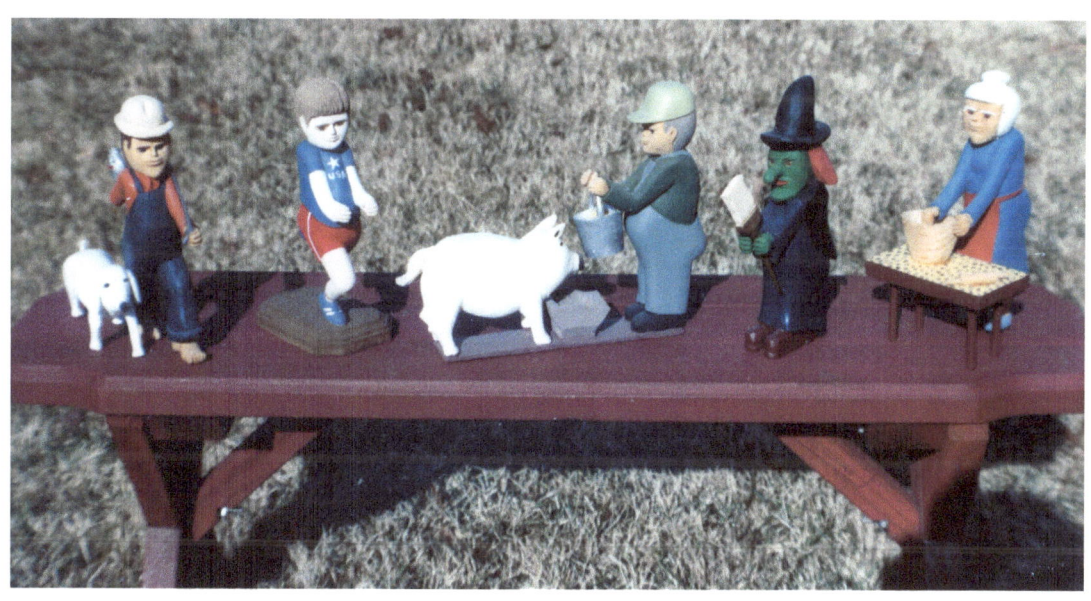

Burlon Craig (1914 - 2002) was a master of the Catawba Valley alkaline glaze pottery tradition. He made utilitarian stoneware and became known for his face jugs. He was named a National Endowment for the Arts Heritage Fellow in 1984 and received the North Carolina Heritage Award in 1991.

It's a little satisfaction when you burn a nice kiln full and set it out and look at it. You jus' have to have a little pride about it. I enjoy seein' it, and I enjoy workin' with it.

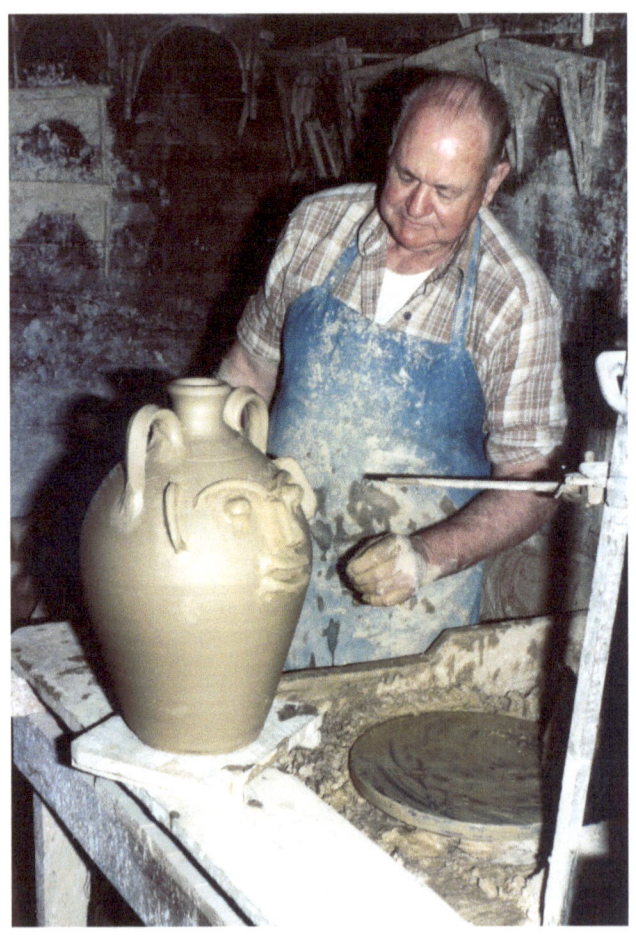

Interviewed in Vale, NC: March 13 and 27, 1984.

Burlon Craig

BURLON CRAIG - POTTER

I really don't know whether I was born in Lincoln County or Catawba County. Back then they didn't keep a birth certificate. But my father wrote down the date I was born — April 21st, 1914. There was ten boys and every one had a sister, that would make eleven. They are all still a livin' but one. [My Daddy] farmed and was a Church of God preacher.

I went to school the first couple of years at Ridge Academy at Cat Square.[1] Me and another boy used to run off from school on lunch hour to watch Ol' Man Bass[2] turn[3]. He was workin' at the Leonard[4] place, jus' a little way back from the school. That's the first contact I had with the pottery. That fascinated me, a watchin' him pull clay up. I jus' couldn't see how he could do that.

After we moved from Lincoln County, I went to Banoak [School]. How many years did I go? Not many. I'm ashamed to tell you. Not many. I helped farm, then I decided there must be some other way to make a living besides pickin' cotton. I can remember my back hurtin' so bad from pickin' cotton. Now you talk about something rough, that pickin' cotton was rough. So when I got old enough to work, I had a chance to help Ol' Man Lynn[5] out makin' pottery. I got started with him by bringing one of my Dad's mules down here to ground the clay[6]. He didn't keep a mule. He'd give me 25 cents to bring the mule. I was about 10 or 11 years old, old enough to put the gears on the mule and look after him. That was a lot of fun for me.

We had a lot of wood, too. My Daddy had a yard of cut lumber, the slabs that [the potters] used back then to burn[7]. I'd cut the tops of trees up into cord wood and we'd make logs into slabs. Ol' Man Lynn wanted me to go into partners with him then, wanted to use up that wood. It was hard to get good wood. So I started in his shop. I started in the fall — really serious, and then by spring I was makin' some stuff to sell. I was about 13 [years old].

I never knowed [Jim Lynn] to ever make a face jug. Some of the other [potters] did. I think Ol' Man Bass made the first face jug I ever saw. I've heard a good many of the ol' timers[8] talk about

---

1 A community in Lincoln County
2 Will Bass, a potter
3 To make pottery
4 Lawrence Leonard, a potter who had a shop
5 Jim Lynn, a potter. The area of Catawba/Lincoln counties where Mr. Craig lived (his home was on the county lines), was the location of several potters who worked in the alkaline glaze tradition.
6 The mule was harnessed to a pug mull used to grind the clay
7 To fire a kiln of ware
8 Old potters who were living

the face jugs, and they said it originated in Africa. They claimed they made 'em in Africa and put 'em on the graves to keep the evil spirits away. Then when they brought the slaves over here, they started makin' 'em, the natives over here made 'em. And some of the ol' timers could remember, when I was a boy sixty years ago.

I made some [face jugs] ever since I been turnin', but not many [until a few years ago]. When I started, people didn't have any money to buy anything, but only what they could use, like a churn, and they bought the jugs to put molasses in, and milk crocks to put milk in the spring box, before refrigerators. Some would dig a hole in the ground, a milk well, if there was no spring. I've seen my mother make 7 or 8 half pound balls of butter at a time. She'd press it out in a little ol' wooden press. It went to the spring in a special butter crock.

About the time I started or right after, there was some people who'd come up from Charlotte goin' to the mountains. People who had money and cars to travel in. They'd stop and buy a face jug. But you didn't sell any to local people. [The people bought them] would look at [the face jugs] and say, "Ain't that an ugly thing!" The first time I had somebody to look at mine, I jus' knew I wasn't goin' to sell 'em. They kept talkin' how ugly they were, but they wound up buyin' them. But I knowed I done lost a sale there.

Howard Smith[9] pushed me into the snake jug business about eight years ago. If there's anything in the world I hate worse than a snake, I've never seen it. I couldn't think about makin' a snake, but he kept on. I've made a whole lot of snakes.

[In 1934, I married Irene Lindsay]. The first time I ever noticed her, when I thought I was grown up, was on a bus goin' to a commencement exercise at the school house. That was the first time I knew who she was, although I had seen her before.

There wasn't nothin' to work at back then but farmin' and workin' in the saw mill. That's why I got in the pottery business. I had decided I'd rather work in [pottery] than in the sawmill.

When I left Jim and went to work for the Reinhardts[10], I worked by the gallon. I earned two cents a gallon. I got ten cents for turnin' a five gallon piece.

All the potters closed down when the war was goin' on. Harvey [Reinhardt] went to Wilmington to [work in] the ship yards.

---

9 An art dealer
10 Harvey and Enoch Reinhardt, brothers and potters

Burlon Craig

They did draft me. When I went for the first time and taken the examination, there was a Marine Colonel, an Army Colonel, and a Navy Commander a sittin' there. They asked me all kinds of questions, asked me, "How do you feel about goin' over there and fightin'?" I said "Well, I think somebody's goin' to have to do some fightin' or they're goin' to take the country over. Jus' as well be me as somebody else. I'll do what I can. It won't be much, what one man can do, but I'll do what I can." That's the answer I gave them, which is the way I felt. They looked me over and said I had my choice — Marines, Navy or the Army. I taken the Navy.

[I served] in the Pacific — Australia, New Guinea, Solomons[11], all over the Pacific. I was a gunner, first loader on a 3 inch gun. I crossed the Pacific Ocean ten times.

The longest I was at sea was 32 days. We went from San Francisco to Townsville, Australia. [I was on] what they called an attack transport, we hauled troops for an invasion. The first two trips I made was [on an] ammunition ship. I was glad to get off of that thing for I seen one of them blowed up. We was runnin' a convoy down in Solomon Islands. The gun crew had to stand watch about an hour before sundown, then about an hour before the sun got up and you could see good. I was standin' on deck one mornin' a watchin'. A Jap submarine slipped in there. We was runnin' out on the edge of the convoy — in the center they had the troop [ships]. They were protectin' the men. We had destroyers and I think one battleship in one convoy. [The submarine] torpedoed [the other ammunition ship]. I was standin' a lookin' at this ship when it happened. It looked like that ship jumped up in the middle and fell apart. When [the torpedo] hit that thing, all the ammunition below the water line went off — split the ship in two. Nobody got off that ship. Nobody.

The last ship I was on was fast. How come we crossed the ocean so many times was we was fast. If they needed something in a hurry, they sent us after it. They run us back from the Philippines one time for a railroad outfit. They was a trainin' a railroad outfit to take over that little dinky train that run out of Manila up in the mountains. They sent us after it. And they needed a rocket outfit. We got the honor of comin' back and gettin' them. That rocket outfit was when they invaded Northern Luzon Island. We put them ashore [with] a heavy artillery outfit. We even had their sub spotter plane, we put it all on the beach.

The day I came in from the west coast [at the end of the war], I come into Hickory on a bus. I run into Enoch Reinhardt at the bus station. Enoch said that Harvey was a wantin' to sell this place.[12] He said "I'd like to see you get it."

---

11 Solomon Islands
12 The Craig's lived on the farm with the pottery shop they purchased from Harvey Reinhardt.

[When I bought it from Harvey] in 1945, the shop was here and ever thing jus' like it is now. Harvey and Enoch built the kiln[13] here and one out at Enoch's place. They made the brick. They got the dirt down here in my pasture.

They had bought several kinds of fire bricks, but had trouble with it. They got the dirt, but it had enough clay in it to hold it together. They experimented with the brick when they burned a kiln of ware. They made a hundred and twenty thousand bricks, hand molded. Stacked them where the fire would go between them and they burned them their selves.

Them [Reinhardt] boys was something else. They'd tackle anything, including each other. They carried a gun for one another for a long time. Then one day they joined the Jehovah Witness [group]. [The Jehovah Witnesses] put up a little tent across the road from Enoch's place. Two preachers come in and was a preachin'. [The brother's] mother Mary lived over here and she come [to the tent]. I was there. The preachers were gettin' ready to have the service. Mary said, "I want you to pray for my boys. They're gone to kill one another." A few days later they both got religion and throwed their guns away. Then's when they went into the pottery business together. I suppose they fell out later when they busted up[14]. They only made pottery for seven years in the thirties.

The first [furniture] job I had was at Broyhill's, then I went to North Hickory.[15] But I burnt more kilns then than I do now. I was makin' churns and jugs, and I wasn't a goin' through all this puttin' the faces on. It takes longer to put the face on than it does to make the piece.

I'd turn awhile of an evenin' when I wasn't farmin.' We were haulin' a lot of [my pottery] off, a sellin' to stores like Stamey Company[16] and hardware stores like Boyce Hardware in Hickory.

Back in the fifties, Dale (one of the boys[17]) and myself had a shop [to sell pottery to tourists. It was located on Highway 18 toward the mountains.] I went down [to Randolph County[18]] and bought several pick-up loads of pottery from Ol' Man C. C. Cole. He told me some things that helped me [with pottery making]. And I bought some from the Owens. The way we worked it at first, [Dale would] go stay [at the shop,] through the week, then we'd go stay the weekend. Then he went into the Army. But I couldn't take that seven days [a week]. I made right smart unglazed flower pots and pitchers for the shop. They sold pretty good.

---

13 The kiln is a ground hog type, so called because it is constructed partially underground.

14 Dissolved the pottery business

15 Two local furniture factories. Mr. Craig worked nearly 20 years in furniture factories.

16 At Fallston, N.C.

17 The Craigs have five children, 3 boys and 2 girls.

18 In Central N.C., the location of several pottery-making families, including the Coles and the Owens.

Burlon Craig

[To make pottery], you've got to get the right kind of clay. You've got to know what you want. You've got to dig that clay. The best clay is just in certain areas [of the bank] of the South Fork of the Catawba River. Where I'm a gettin' clay, we got it back when I worked over at Seth Ritchie's[19]. Seth got it there. Different people own the farm now.

When you dig [the clay] it's in big lumps. I like for it to lay over the winter. It helps it turn better if it'll freeze and thaw. You've got to soak that clay good before you put it in the mill to grind it. I break me off what I think I want to grind and take my hand in the water bucket and [splash] water over it. If it's thoroughly soaked, it gets soft.

Then you put it in the mill and grind it [to get] all the lumps out of it. This lady down in Lincolnton was a writin' something about me in the paper,[20] and she said [I used a mule] until my last mule died, but that's not right. I've used the tractor [motor to turn the mill] most of the time since I've been here. But I used the mule a little bit. I've made I don't know how many clay mills before I made this one I've got out here. I made some I didn't use long.

You keep [the clay] covered up good, and take them sacks[21] off and sprinkle water over it ever once in a while, you can keep it for years maybe.

Outside of your halves and one gallon stuff, it'll average around four pounds [of clay] to the gallon. I use twenty pounds for a five gallon [piece] and forty pounds a ten gallon. But to make a one gallon piece you want about six pounds. I work[22] the clay [to get the air and rocks out.] This [kick wheel] come from the ol' Hilton[23] shop over at Oyama. It's a heavy wheel — you want something pretty heavy. You get it a turnin', then it helps you keep it goin'. When you 're formin' your ball and truin'[24] your clay, you don't have to kick yourself to death.

The first step is to put it on the lathe, center it, then use the ball opener[25] to make the bottom. On the small stuff, I don't use it. But you can make a small bottom by hand, probably up to a gallon size — on a big piece, you've got to have a uniform bottom, if you don't, it'll be damaged in the fire.

---

19 Another local potter who was working when Mr. Craig started out. Mr. Craig is the last traditional potter in the area. Most of the others stopped when World War II started.
20 Newspaper
21 Burlap sacks cover the pile of ground clay in the potting shop
22 Knead
23 Ernest Hilton pottery
24 Centering
25 A wooden device

Then you've got to dry [the pottery], then glaze it. Let it dry again so the glaze'll soak in. I use glass, clay slips and ashes in my [glaze]. You have to pulverize[26] [the glass] and sift it through a medium sifter. Then I grind it between two rocks, like old cornmeal. Then I mix it. When I get [the glaze] to the thickness I want, I dip [the pottery] down in it, and tilt the mouth so the glaze'll run inside, then turn it a complete roll. Drain [the glaze] out of the jug. I take a small brush and knock the glaze off the bottom where it sits in the sand[27].

[To burn the kiln I use pine], all pine. Oh, you might use a few poplar or oak [pieces] mixed with it, but not in the last two hours. The pine is the best, it makes more of a blast[28]. Your blaze and heat'll go on through your kiln better. You've got to have blast. [It takes] right close to three cords [of wood, and about ten hours to burn a kiln].

I like [the interest in my pottery] because I can get more out of what I'm doin'. Back when [we were selling to hardware stores] we got a dollar a gallon. If all this had happened back in my young days, by now I could have been a rich man. For I could turn out a lot then, not like it is now. I [used to] turn about 25 five gallon pieces in a day in churns and jugs. If I really worked, I could almost turn a kiln full in a week.

At first I dreaded [people coming to talk to me]. I'm the type that never was one much for meetin' strangers, goin' up to a stranger and talkin' to him. I've got now to where I don't think anything about it. It's part of the job. Like somebody watchin' me turn, it use to bother me — I got out of part of that when I went to the fairs[29].

Irene'd fuss sometime [when visitors come] because I don't dress up and change clothes — I didn't want to be like that ol' man in Alabama they tell about, sayin' he'd come out to turn with a white shirt and neck tie on. I hardly ever dress up that way on Sunday.

It might sound corny, but it's a little satisfaction when you burn a nice kiln full and set it out and look at it. You jus' have to have a little pride about it. I enjoy seein' it, and I enjoy workin' with it. I don't guess I'd be satisfied without it. Even when I had to work at something else to make a livin', I still enjoyed it.

---

26 Mr. Craig uses a glass beater to crush old glass. The glass beater is powered by water flow at a nearby stream.

27 The bottom of the kiln is sand

28 The last two hours of a kiln burn is called a blast off, when a lot of wood is added to the fire, creating a very intense blaze.

29 Agricultural fairs in Cleveland County, Charlotte, and Raleigh that included craft demonstrations

Burlon Craig

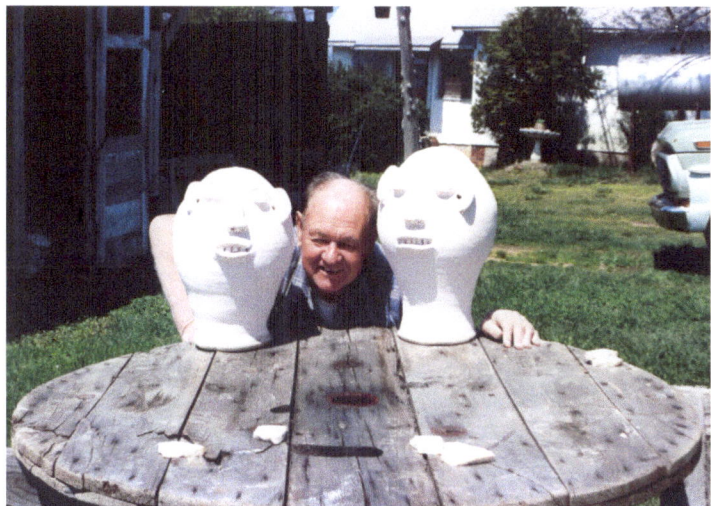

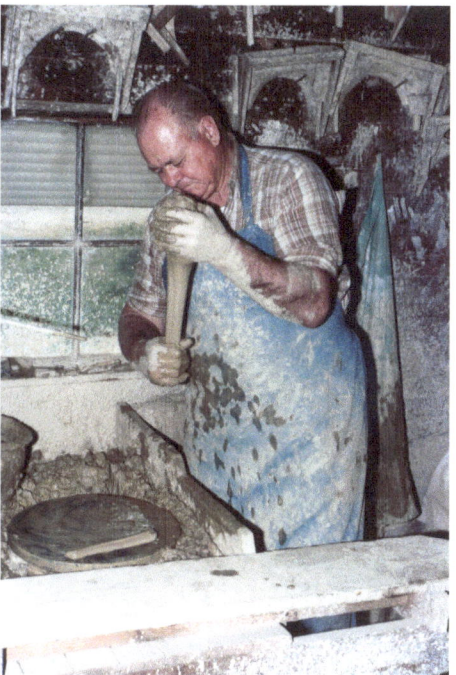

Burlon Craig with unfired face wig stands

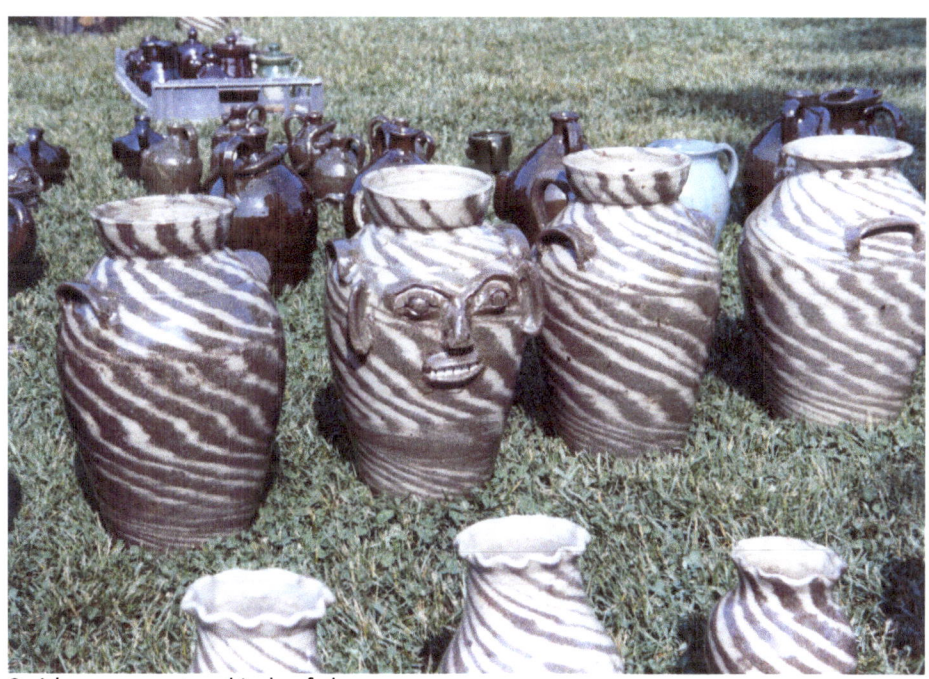

Swirl ware uses two kinds of clay.

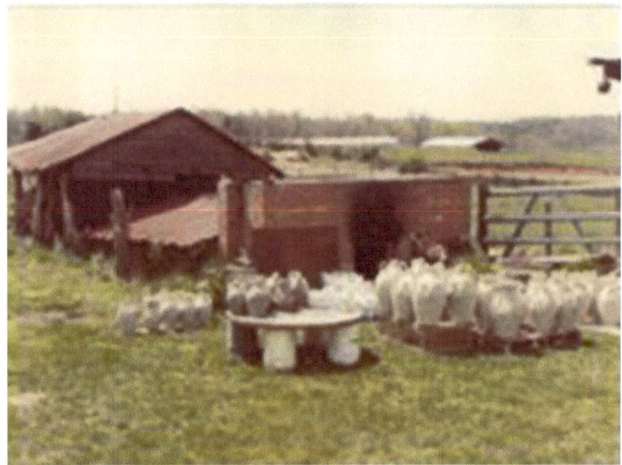

Greenware awaiting placement in the kiln

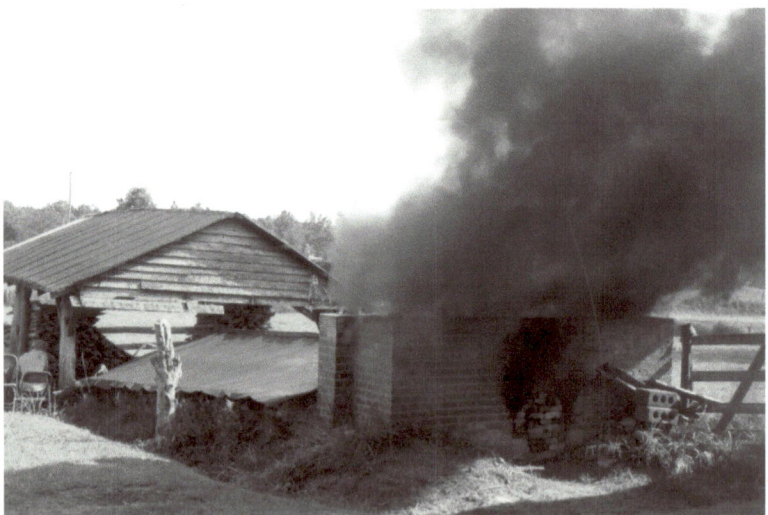

The kiln at blast off

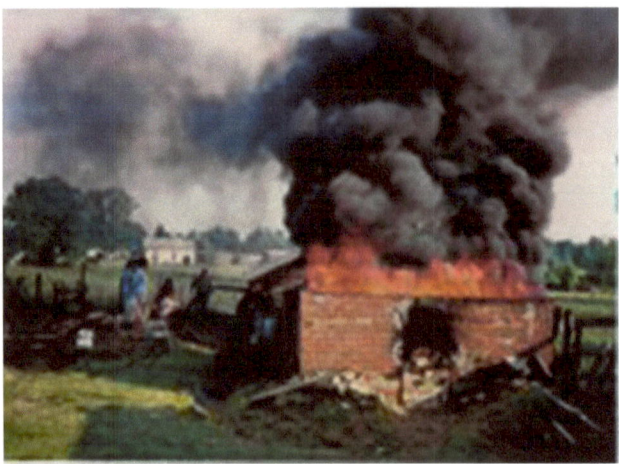

Blast off during the firing process

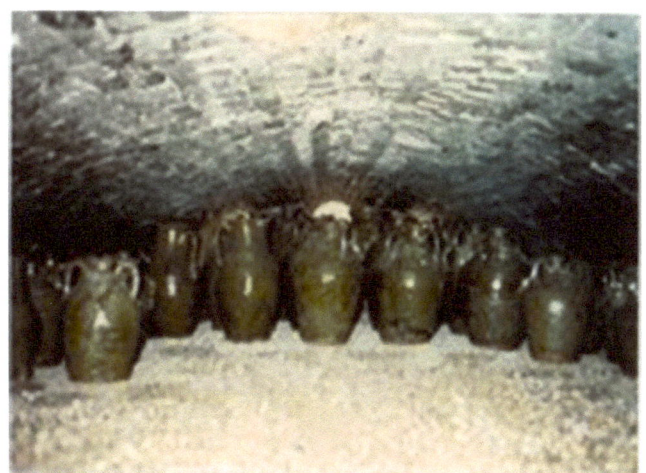

Fired ware waiting to be removed from kiln

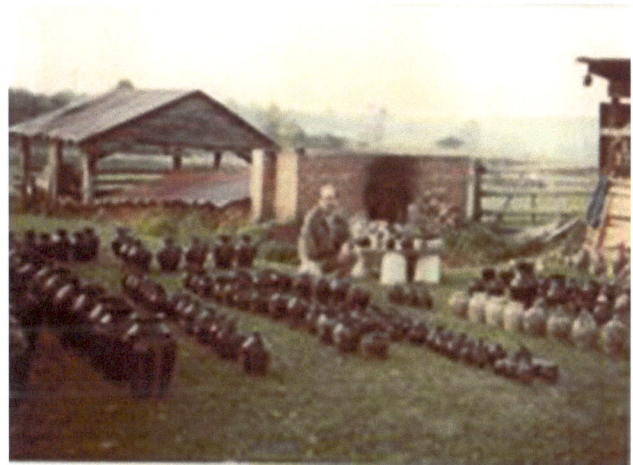

Pottery lined up for a kiln sale

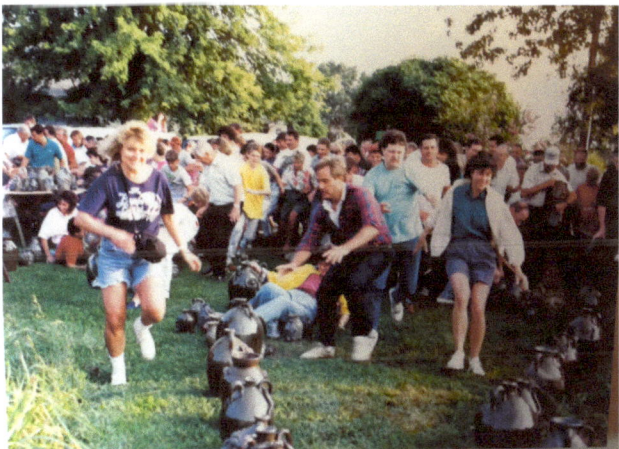

Running for pottery at a kiln sale

Elenora Hamilton (1911 – 2003) returned to her birthplace on Ocracoke Island in the 1970s after retiring as a hairdresser. She began painting, inspired by a fortune teller who told her to paint. Her subject matters reflect her childhood memories on the Outer Banks, with coastal village scenes and charming interiors.

Most of the things I paint from my mind of my childhood. Some things I leave out, but most things I put in, especially those things that mean something to me.

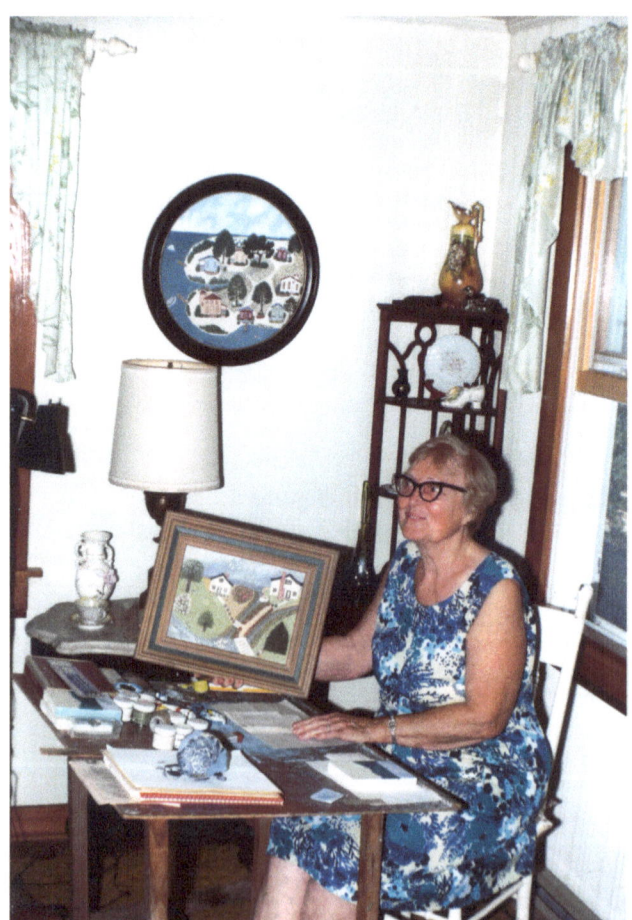

Holding her first painting.

Interviewed on Ocracoke Island, NC: July 11, 1984

Elenora Hamilton

Elenora Hamilton - Painter

I was born on the island[1] in 1911 at home. They didn't have anything but midwives then —
no doctors. My mother's family was here from 1759, and my father's from 1756. The whole
island was sold to a Howard at first, and the next year the Howards sold half of it to a Williams,
and that is the Williams we are. My father's name was Horatio Jones Williams — quite a
name, and my mother's name was Virginia Thomas O'Neal. My father's father was named
James Nelson Williams. I had a brother and four sisters. One's dead now. A nice size family.

My father worked in the Coast Guard. They had to police the beach in those days. If you had
a horse, you rode the horse. But if you didn't have a horse, you had to walk all the way to the
other station, which was up at the other end of the island. The Coast Guard looked for ship
wrecks or people in distress. They had the lighthouse[2] but they still had to go up to the other
end of the island because they couldn't see from this area. There was a lot of ship wrecks, and
a lot of people were saved on account of the Coast Guard.

When I was growing up on Ocracoke, they didn't have any ferries. The only access we had to
the outside world was by boat. There were two freight boats that left Ocracoke and went to
Washington[3], and they also took passengers. And then the mail boat would go to Morehead
City at first, and then years later it went to Atlantic, then years later it went to Cedar Island[4],
before we got a ferry. From this end of the island to Hatteras[5] there was no highway or
anything. If you went to Hatteras, you had to go by boat. But then there was nothing much
at Hatteras at that time.

There was a hotel here. The hotel was right where the present Coast Guard station is, and
it burned in 1903. So this Coast Guard station has been built since then. It was a hundred
room hotel, and three different pleasure boats would come and put people out. They had horses
to pull a wagon with seats on each side, and they had a cover over it. They would pull the wagon
to the beach. It was on a track like a railroad. There was a built track, and my father worked
there when he was young for a while. He said they were the best-dressed people. I mean well-to-
do people, because that was all that could afford to come here, I guess. It was so hard to get to, it
took days to get here. I have a picture of that hotel. I hope to paint a picture of it someday.

---

1 Ocracoke Island, located at the southern end of North Carolina's Outer Banks
2 Ocracoke Lighthouse was built in 1823, and is North Carolina's oldest lighthouse.
3 Washington, North Carolina
4 A small community on the mainland. It now serves as a state ferry landing.
5 Hatteras is a town located on the southern tip of Hatteras Island, thus separated from Ocracoke by water.

I had a wonderful mother and father. On last Mother's Day, I said to myself that I was very happy that my mother was my mother. I think that is the greatest compliment you can pay a mother.

Poppa had chickens and we had a cow and he had a horse. I can remember we had a shed, and I would cut wood myselfI was always the tomboy. Poppa dug a hole and put sawdust in it, and in the summertime the freight boats would bring ice to the island. He would get a block of ice and bring it home in the horse and cart, and put it in this hole, and cover it up with sawdust so it wouldn't melt, and put it underground. We would have enough ice to last until the next freight boat came. That's how we kept our food and had ice too. Poppa had two lovely gardens. Most everybody raised their own vegetables. We had the best sweet potatoes. A lot of people think you can't grow anything in this sand, but you can if you do it right. My daddy used to put seaweed in the rows to keep grass from growing, and in due time it made the soil rich. His gardens were beautiful. I used to piddle in his gardens a lot.

We had water that ran right by here, and I used to sail sailboats in that little stream of water when I was a little girl. It was about a foot deep, I guess. Everybody kept their yards clean and their fences white washed. And the trees in the yard would be cut and white washed. It was quite pretty.

We went to church three times on Sunday — morning services, Sunday school at two o'clock, and night service. That was all there was to do. Nobody worked on Sunday in those days. There were two churches here, Southern Methodists and Northern Methodists. After one church was damaged, they tore them down and made one church, the one we have now.

There were no newspapers, no T.V., no radios during my childhood, then later on they had radios. But the islands were just outside of everything. They may have voted, I don't remember. I guess they voted.

We didn't have any cars, and we didn't have any crime, and everybody loved everybody. I think that's the reason I'm back, because I had such a lovely, happy childhood, really. It's quaint. Your parents didn't have to worry about you getting into trouble. They had little quaint roads which I loved. They had horse and cart roads too, but they also had little paths that you could run from one person's house to another, and to the store. They were just little paths that you would make by constantly going over it. Very quaint. Peaceful.

We had quite a few hurricanes. The first year I built myhouse we had five. But no one ever lost a home here. I don't know that anybody has lost their life in a hurricane, not during my

Elenora Hamilton

mother's and father's generation anyway. Before the Park Service[6] built up the sand fences, if the ocean came up, it just came right over the island, and when it went down, it went down. The same way with the sound. But now it backs up. It gets to the sand fences then it sort of backs up. Notice how close our highway is to the beach. There's going to be an inlet cut through if they don't watch out. Nothing they can do about it.

When a big storm came the people would move all the furniture upstairs if they knew it was going to be a bad one. They didn't have any way of knowing other than just having a feeling about what they should do. Now the water never went in our house but one time, and I think that was the '44 storm. I wasn't here. I was married, living in Richmond. But the water did go in just a little bit, but some of the houses had a foot or foot-and-a-half in them. After that most everybody raised their houses up two feet higher because they didn't want to have to go through that trouble again. An' I can understand why. They tell me it was a mess.

When I got about 14 with my red hair and freckles, I didn't go out very much, not in the daytime, because I used freckle cream. I'd be just as white as a lily. My mother used to say, "Honey, if you just go out and get a little sunburn. You just don't look like the rest of the people around here." Oh, I had the most beautiful skin, didn't have any freckles because I used all that freckle cream. But now I don't care about freckles. It doesn't bother me. I don't have as many as I had when I was a little girl anyway.

When I was 14 and I left the island, I thought everybody in the world was honest. I didn't know people were bad. I really didn't. We never learned about murder and all that mess. It just wasn't in our thinking. Nobody had ever done such a thing down here.

If you died, the neighbors would come in and shroud you and bury you. You weren't embalmed or anything. They would wait until the next day probably. Now it's just like everywhere else. They send your body away, and you come back and have a big funeral. Everything's gotten a little modern.

If anybody got sick, they didn't have any doctors or nurses here. The people of the island would take time about sitting up over a person, day and night. They would have about an eight hour shift. Just took care of each other. It was beautiful,really. They didn't know much about medicine. They didn't send their people to the hospital. Most people died from old age. They didn't die young here. Just from old age.

When I was growing up the schools weren't very good. They would take most anybody to

---

6   Most of Ocracoke is designated national Seashore and is administered by the National Park Service.

teach. Anybody on the island who had any education at all could teach. But my father thought we deserved more than that, I reckon. I went away when I was 14 to be educated. I went to Misenheimer in the upper part of North Carolina. It's Pheiffer College now. I only went there one year then my father transferred us to Washington, North Carolina. Washington Collegiate Institute was the name of the boarding school.

I was nineteen when I finished in Washington, then I went to Richmond and studied to be a beautician. I met Norton in Richmond. I was about 21 years old when I married him. We lived in Richmond 50 years. He was an auditor. He really didn't have the schooling for it. He got him a book and that was all he needed, he said. That was his job, and he did very well. Norton Hamilton is of the Alexander Hamilton family. He really is.

I was a beautician until I moved here. That was the only way I could get out of it, to tell the truth. When I was forty, I sold my beauty parlor because I didn't want to leave my children. Then I had just one room at home, in fact, my recreation room was my beauty parlor. And I would work while the children were in school. Ten years before I moved here, I moved out of Richmond ten more miles, thinking nobody would come. I waited on my customers, some of them forty-five years. They were real friends. They weren't just customers. They'd come out and spend half a day — eat lunch with me. My husband said, "You're making a lot of money — ha!" But you know when you've been waiting on somebody forty-five years, they become more than customers.

I came back to Ocracoke every summer to visit my mother and father. However, when my father got married again, I didn't like his wife much, so I didn't come back for eight years. That was during the second world war. They didn't want you to come back. They didn't want anybody who didn't have to come, to come. That was not my excuse though.

There was a lot of activity here during the war. In fact, this lake[7] was dug out for the biggest natural submarine base the government had. It was right here at Ocracoke. There were seven hundred sailors stationed here all the time. This area was built up with a hospital, recreation, and barracks, all from here on to the Coast Guard station. Ammunition dumps were up all by the concrete roads. They made these cinder block things[8], then covered them up with sand — camouflaged. That's how we got highways, really, was during that time. They had to build highways to the ammunition dumps. Later people bought the land and tore the bunkers down. However, they used the blocks.

---

7 Silver Lake
8 Ammunition bunkers

Elenora Hamilton

Norton came back with me in the summers. Then I built the house 35 years ago to rear my children here in the summer. We stayed at Pappa's three or four years before I built it. You know how it is when you have growing children with old people. They can't stand too much noise. My children enjoyed being here, so my father gave me the land. We used the house until they got grown, then I rented it for about two-thirds of the summer, then I'd have it for my own use. The rest of the time I stayed at my daddy's.

We retired six years ago[9]. Norton and I decided to come here to live for good. When we moved we had so much stuff. This house was furnished. It was in December when we sold the Richmond house, and we had to be out in six weeks. Snow was on the ground for two weeks, so we didn't have a chance to get rid of anything. I did give our daughter who had just bought a house, a lot of furniture. But we had a big, big house. So when we came here, I had to build this garage[10] to store everything, and decide what I wanted to put in the house. Then I had to have a sale, furniture and all. It took me about two years to sell all that stuff I didn't want. Now I enjoy it so much, I buy when I go to Richmond. My daughters (both my daughters teach in Richmond and I have two lovely grandsons) go to estate sales and buy for me from time to time.

People enjoy it. They come and mill around. Of course I have new things and old things, antique things. I have few antiques now. I had quite a few at first, but they went right quick. Those crocheted tablecloths are nice. You don't see them much anymore. I sell a lot of buttons. Buttons are very expensive. People collect them. I have all kinds of odd buttons. It's just fun. Meet a lot of nice people. That's how I sell most of my art, really, from the back yard sale. I have a garage full of paintings. That's where most of my art is.

My daughters' names are Elenora Marsha Hamilton and Gail Thomas Hamilton. They are lovely girls. We usually stay with them seven weeks in the winter, three weeks in the fall and three weeks in the spring. The children insist on our going. But after you move here, you get so you don't want to leave for any length of time. Maybe two weeks, but seven weeks is too long for me to be gone. I begin to get homesick. It's strange. I lived in Richmond fifty years, but this has always been home. And I always knew I'd retire here.

You really want to know why I started painting? This is the truth. This doctor friend of ours in Richmond had a lady visitor from New York named Dr. Alston. She could read your aura. He invited several people to come — I was one — and she read our auras. She said, "Lady, you should paint." I said, "Lady, I can't draw a straight line." And I can't. She said, "I don't care. You should paint. By all means, you should go out and get paints and mix them because you'll

---

9 1978
10 Mrs. Hamilton now uses the garage for her shop.

mix colors that nobody else mixes." Everybody that buys my art says the colors are so different.

Well, I didn't pay any attention to that woman at all. Twelve or fifteen years passed. I had this vase I wanted Ann, the doctor's wife, to paint. The flowers on it had worn off. She was an artist. So I took it by her house and asked her to paint it. She said, "Well, I'm sorry - There's my paints and there's my brushes. You paint it yourself. Dr. Alston said you should paint, so you just as well start." I said, "Ann, I can't do that." She said, "Well, try." I did it, and I was very pleased.

I went out and bought twenty five dollars — in those days, twenty five dollars' worth of paints was right much worth of paints and brushes. I went home and painted my first picture. I painted sixteen pictures in five weeks. Some of them are just as good as what I do today. That is true. I've been painting ever since.

I would never have started if that woman hadn't told me to. And I would have never started if Ann hadn't pushed me into it. So I guess it was just meant for me to do it.

I started painting in July 1973. I won my first blue ribbon, which I was quite pleased with, in Richmond. There were at least 400 paintings in the art show. I won that in July, 1975. Sometimes I'd go for a year and not paint in Richmond, then I'd wonder if I could. I've painted more since I've been here because I've had more time. I still don't have too much time to do it.

The first picture I made was two houses, one of them represented my grandmother's house. I, as a child, had to take milk to my grandmother every day. I had long red hair. I painted myself going across this little bridge taking the milk. That memory was what triggered the painting. I've been told by several artists that teach art, that the painting was very good. That was the first painting, and I didn't have anything to go by.

I've never taken any lessons. I've been advised not to. I can't draw. You should have seen me try to draw that dog's picture in that painting. I won the blue ribbon. I couldn't draw the dog to save my life. I tried and tried and tried. But I can paint it. I don't know why, but I can. I think that's very unusual. I don't take the ruler and draw things like a lot of people. I seem to be able to judge the spaces.

Most of the things I paint from my mind of my childhood. Some things I leave out, but most things I put in, especially those things that mean something to me, like the hammock in that picture. My daddy made it out of barrel staves. My mother would give me a quilt to put in it, and I'd go to sleep out there in the daytime. It meant a great deal to me.

Elenora Hamilton

We didn't have access to stores. The people here, especially my father, could do anything. He could build houses, boats, just do anything. If you wanted something, just ask and if he felt like doing it, he would do it. So he made me that hammock and swings. We had swings, two on the front and one on the back. Because people at Ocracoke used to like to swing and sing when they were children.

I have several more memories that I want to paint. I don't know when I'll get to it, but I want to paint that old hotel. Also, I want to paint where my children used to swim, with all the driftwood that was on the shore. We used to hang our towels on it.

When I start to paint, I have to be quiet. I can't paint with anybody. I can paint and look at T.V. once in a while — a musical or something of that sort. My husband doesn't talk to me when I'm painting unless he has to. I have to concentrate on what I remember.

I used oils up until about three weeks ago. I've made one painting of acrylic. I've just started using water colors on a painting that's already drawn. That is Blackbeard's house[11], the only thing I ever drew. I don't enjoy watercolors. I enjoy oils. If I was going to put much money in a painting, it would be oils, because all you got to do is get one of the others wet, and it's gone. The oils will last. Now the acrylics — I don't know anything about acrylics. I'm just getting so I paint shells[12] and little stuff to earn just enough money to buy my canvas and paints.

I thoroughly enjoy painting. I really do enjoy it. Between October and December and then when I come back from Richmond the first of March or April, that's when I do most of my work. Now the poem I wrote, I paint most of those[13] any time. They're not hard to do, and they sell very good.

Everybody loves the painting of the houses — Ocracoke as it was 60 or 70 years ago. And my mother's kitchen. Those are my two famous pictures. The last painting I did I love. I have very few colors in it. It's mostly grey, blue, and green. It's very pretty. It has a serenity to it. Now the first ferry that ever came to Ocracoke, that painting means a great deal to me because we used to come on that ferry, and I used to think it would break into before I got home. It only held two cars. But that is how we got our ferry from Hatteras. Frazier Peale built it by hand. He had it for a year or two. He was so busy that the state took it over. Now we have fine ferries, one every forty minutes.

---

11 Mrs. Hamilton refer to prints of a drawing of Blackbeard's house. She sells them as note cards and hand-colored prints.

12 Sometimes she paints pictures on sea shells and wooden items.

13 She hand-paints a copy of a poem she wrote.

How do I feel about my paintings? It's just a part of me really. I have so much love within me about this island that people can feel it. This man bought a picture said, "There's so much love in this picture, I can hardly put it down." You can't imagine the love I put in that picture.

All my paintings, I enjoy painting them. If I paint something and I don't like it, I paint over it. It's got to suit me. I've got to like it. I'm not painting for anybody else. I'm painting for myself.

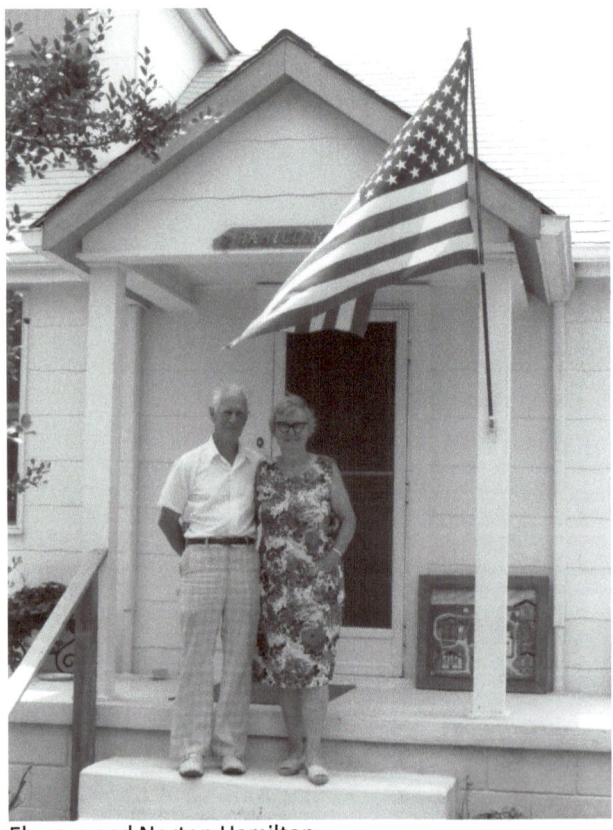

Elenora and Norton Hamilton

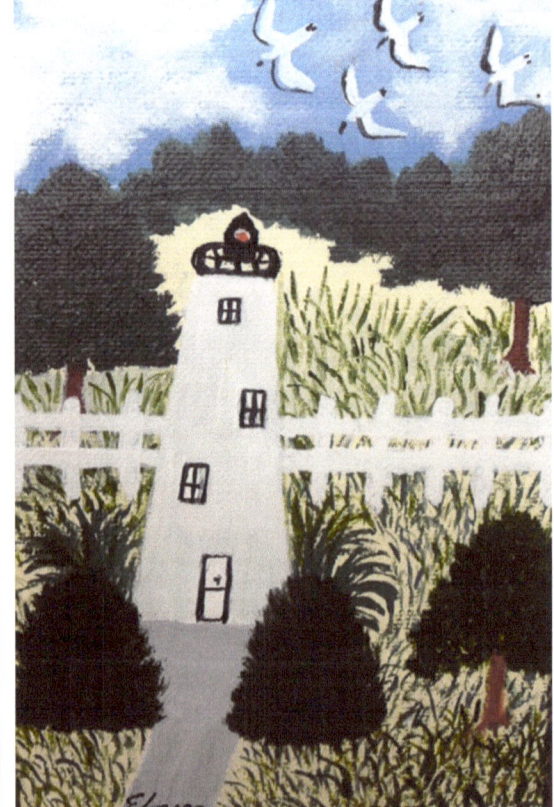

Elenora Hamilton

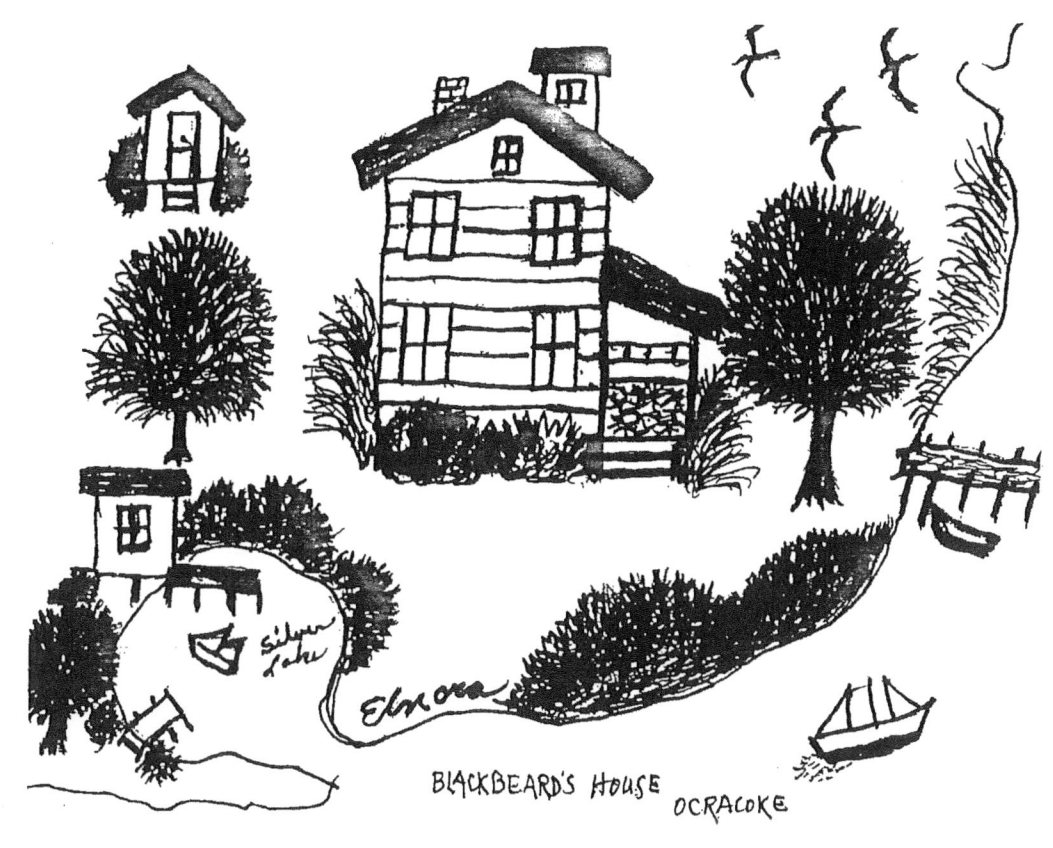

BLACKBEARD'S HOUSE OCRACOKE

BLACKBEARD'S HOUSE AT SPRINGERS POINT,
OCRACOKE, N.C.

THE SAYING WAS HE LOOKED OVER
PAMLICO SOUND FROM THE LOOKOUT
ON TOP OF HIS HOUSE. WHEN SHIPS
CAME THROUGH SOUTH POINT INLET
HE SAILED OUT AND ROBBED THEM.

as told to Elnora Hamilton by
her Grandfather

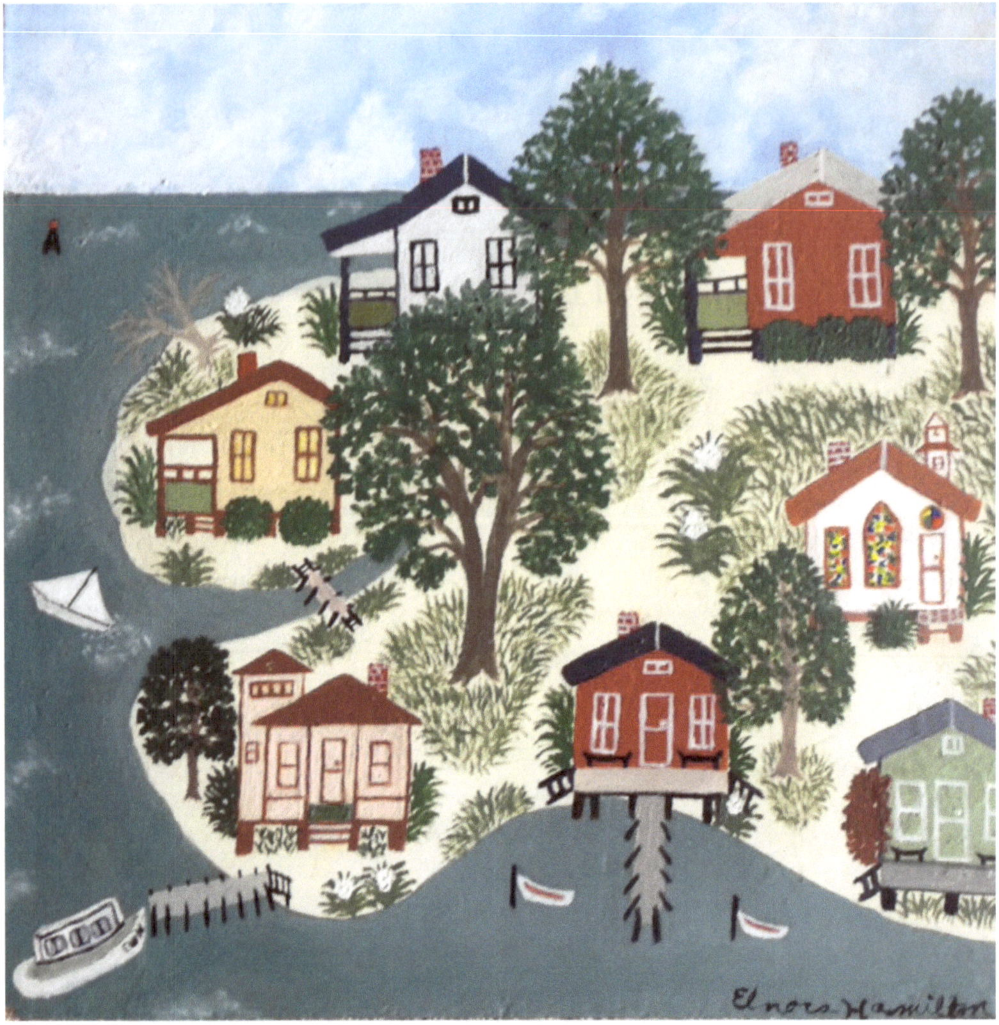

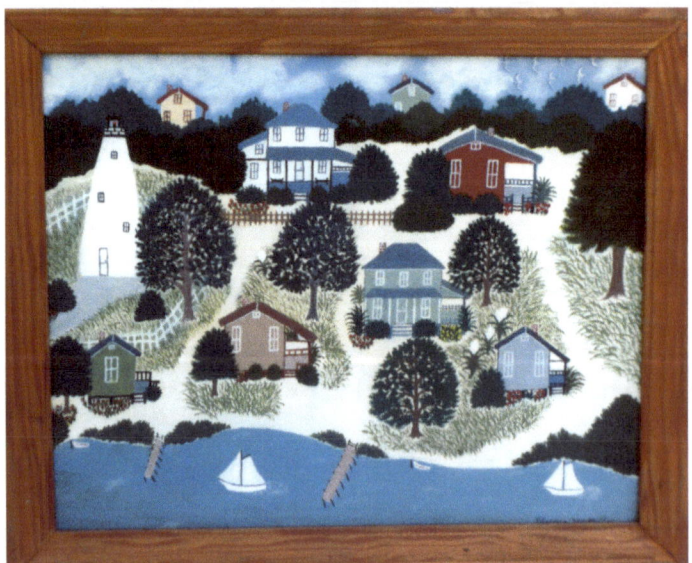

Ocracoke Island scene

Elenora Hamilton

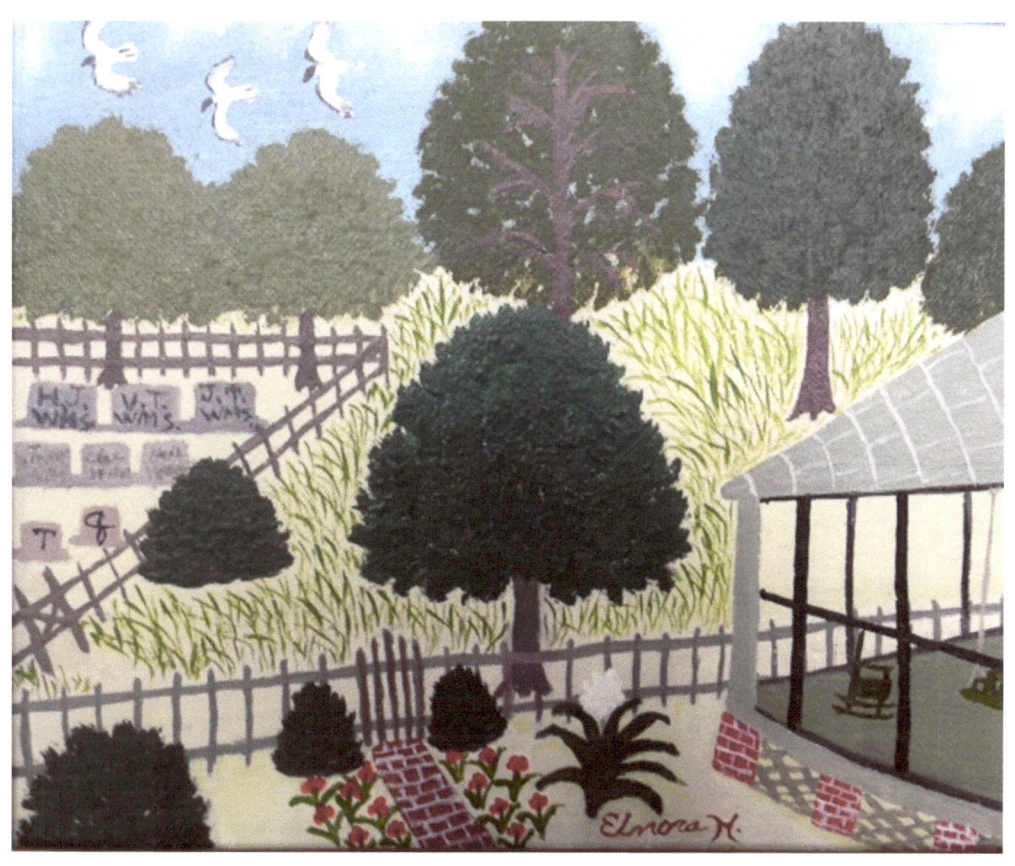

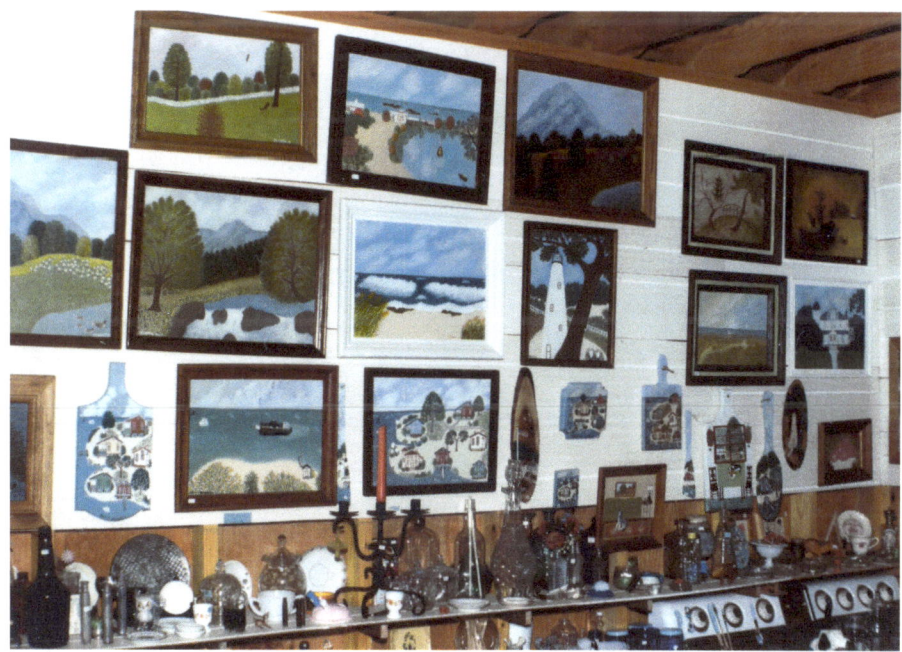

In the garage

Jeff Williams (1958 - ?) is a contemporary folk artist who began carving as a teen, putting his work experience as a carpenter and mechanic to use in crafting sculpture with chainsaw, chisels and files. After making small carvings for himself, he began carving large figural sculptures, one of which was seen in his father's yard by the collector Robert Lynch who encouraged him.

Sculpture work is brain work. You have to really be thinkin'. It's a strain on your brain.

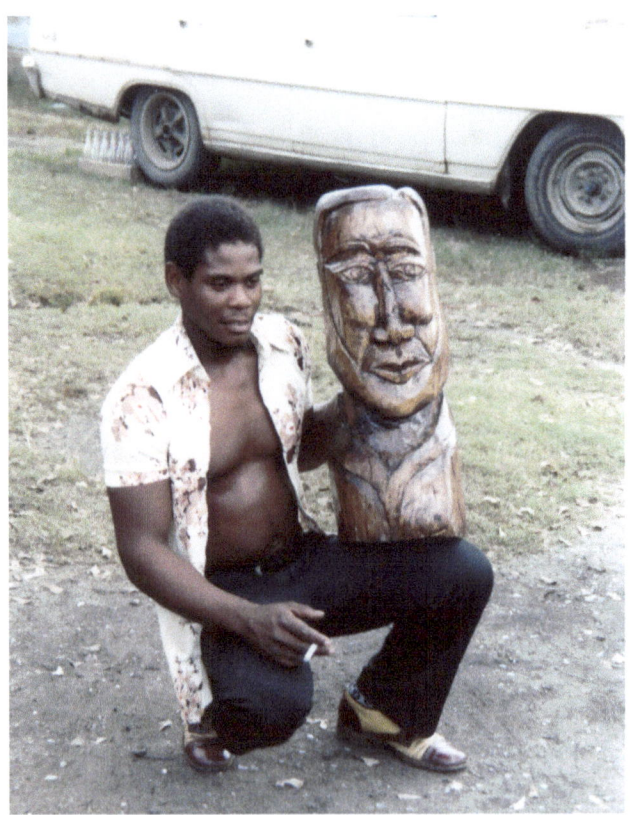

October, 1984

Interviewed in Salemburg, NC: November 1, 1986

Jeff Williams

Jeff Williams - Woodcarver and Sculptor

Yes, [I was born in Salemburg] April 24th, 1958. [My parents are] General Williams and Brenda Ann Williams — [we are] a big family, fourteen — nine boys and five girls. I am the second to the last boy.

I started school in Roseboro, North Carolina, and middle grade school was Roseboro-Salembury, to Lakewood High School. [I graduated] in '75. I used to sit in this class, be bored of the teacher, and draw different things, like write BOY and make a face [out of it], draw a "2" and make a swan. Far years ago there used to be an art class. I so happened one day to do better than the art teacher, and he didn't like it too good.

I used to look in wildlife magazines and see little 'ol drawings like a deer head. You'd draw it and send it off and they would send you back a record on how good you were. They wanted me to take a course in art. I took the course maybe a month or so. I was going to school. Money wasn't too plentiful at the time. I did it for a while, then I just fell apart and went out on my own.

What made me start doin' art work was I was saved in Jesus Christ. One day I had very violent things on my mind. I was just about to do it. I always had bad habits of roamin' through the woods. I was ramblin' in the woods and I seen this certain — some logger had cut this piece out jus' right for me. It was a high stump. (Larry Hackley has this piece[1].) I seen this stump, something about this stump jus' floored me. The stump was waterlogged, full of water, and very heavy. I got it out of the water this day, and maybe a day to two later I had this guy help me get the stump. I brought here and I sawed it out over there. The sun was drawin' the water out.

One day I was tryin' to make something look better around this place.[2] My daddy made me mad. I was broke and I was really violent. So I got mad and I went cryin' about what I wanted to do. These tears was drippin' out of my eyes. I looked at that stump at the time and I seen this style of art. I jus' seen a glow — a little glance — of this style of art on this stump. Right then I jus' forgot about the madness or hatred or whatever. I went out and took a saw, this skill saw, and started cuttin' all these angles. Everything was jus' workin' perfect. Like I would cut this angle like this and this angle like that. I nailed it together and I would think a few minutes and I would cut this piece like that. It was jus' fallin' into place. I built this man sittin' on a stump with a gun. Like a security guard sittin' on a stump. That would be one of the main first pieces in me startin' off doin' this. I seen myself doin' that piece, then I got started. As I sit and watch

---

1 Larry Hackley is a folk art dealer.

2 His parents' home place

this piece, I [was] gettin' really interested. It started with that piece and led onto now. I had a strong interest in that piece.

I found another stump — the angles were cut — and I built these two — one was a black guy and one was a white guy such as I've seen before. The black guy is drinkin.' One is sittin' on one side of the stump and one is sittin' on the other side of the stump. The white guy is sittin' like he's disgusted that he was drunk. The black guy had a bottle to his head, drinkin.'

I jus' started from there and kept goin.' The more interest I put in it, the better I begin to get at what I was doin.' I begin to see the natural look of people, the faces. I got to where I'd be goin' places and see a person with certain face features, and it looked simple. I'd memorize in my head and I'd build this face feature. Now I got to where, if I get this tool I want, I'll go ahead and build it natural, like a natural look face.

What happened, I was jus' bein' pestered a lot by people in my life time. I used to go out and work a job, and I would learn the job fast and quick, very well. The boss would like me, like what I'm doin.' The other guys workin' with me -- the boss would be watchin' me all the time and I wouldn't know it. They'd say I [was] jus' sneakin' around and got a quarter raise.

This job was carpentry work when I first got out of high school. I used to tote[3] a whole house — I mean by pieces. [The boss] give me a hammer. I couldn't drive a nail. I used to beat my thumb. After a while he said, "The only way to make him learn how to drive a nail is to let him beat his thumb to death." I got to where I could drive a nail real good, fancy style. I hit a nail two times and it was in the wood.

From there, [the boss] got where he could trust me, and then it was another raise. He was makin' six dollars.[4] I was makin' five fifty just in a little while, it wasn't long. In carpentry when you get where you can walk the wall [on] a 3 1/2 inch 2 X 4[5], then that's when you're gettin' ready to go make some money. I got to where I could walk the walls, learned how to lay off and put plywood on the roof, different things.

Okay, one day me and the guys, and I got to where I was fancy with the job. Things happened and we fell out.[6] There's a woman in a restaurant, and she was frisky. Every time I'd go to the restaurant she'd frisk with me. Tease me, play with me. The boss man didn't like it. He went to talkin' harsh and hateful to me. That I'd never liked. Bad words.

---

3 Carry
4 Per hour
5 A board size
6 Argued

Jeff Williams

I got mad, and I was so mad I drunk a fifth of liquor, and didn't feel it. I believe I'll rig something for myself where I don't have to have these headaches, messin' with other people. I can kinda half way do things on my own. I made up my mind.

Mainly where I came into art was by anger. People jus' made me mad. I pulled away from a lot of guys that I used to hang around with. Anger was one thing that really drove me into art strongly. It drove me to myself. I got where I wanted to concentrate. I got a strong feelin' for it. It's something I love to do, something I want to do. Sometimes at night when I sleep I see some type of art — like tree limbs nailed together in certain ways. It was a strong piece of art. I jus' started from there. Later on in the years, this guy, a newspaper [man], came out. This guy wanted me to go to Washington and see some sculpture work, like lions. I took the ride with him. I used to paint. I do a lot of paintin', like houses, walls, different things. I went up to Washington and did a lot of paintin' for him. We drove around the town and seen all kinds of different sculptures, like concrete and stuff. Bronze, like horses and men sittin' on 'em. That kinda really stirred up the art in me more. It was big time. I'd love to try to do such as that — put a lot of accent in things I'm doin'.

This lady come along one day. I was feelin' like dirt. I had all my concentration on cuttin' and building. She walked up and touched me on the back, and I jus' about cut myself. She's from Chapel Hill. Her name's — there's a real famous name she's got — ah — Katherine Hepburn. She come along. She seen some pieces I had in the yard. She said, "Do you know what you're doin'?" I said, "Well, the things I got out here, they ain't nothin' at all. They're cartoon men." Folk art. But I didn't know it was folk art. I called them cartoons. She took some pictures. She bought a little funny lookin' man made in this style right here. I did alot of nailin' together. Later on she carne back and bought another piece. That kinda picked me up, made me decide maybe to build bigger and better. It jus' led from there. Step by step, I kept messin' with it.

One of my ol' white friends, he's an ol' man, he wanted this hedgerow cleared up. Somebody had already cut this log down, and it was waterlogged too. I did a lot of strainin' to get it here. I looked at it, and jus' studied. Five, six pack o' beer, sit and lookin', lookin' at this piece o' wood. I would see a feature in this piece of wood. That feature carne to my mind. Most of it I did with an axe. A chain saw is involved, but most of it I did with an axe. I've done aplenty of big pieces. I got where I was puttin' alot of interest in what I was doin'. The big stump of the ol' white man and ol' white lady. They was big logs like this. I got to where I jus' really went into it. I built her a dress with legs. That was takin' strong concentration.

I built a man twelve foot tall. I got a kick out of buildin' this man. It was so high, I put a step ladder up against it to build it. Folks go along and called me sick, pick at me a lot. I drug it around to the front,[7] dug two holes and put it in the ground. Painted it up. People used to come along, be watchin' it, and jus' about run head on into one another. They ain't never seen nothin' like it before. Folk jus' come along to see it, call it junk, all kinds of things.

Most of the people around here, they despise me and what I do. They can't stand to see [people] come around here and talk with me. They don't like that. People come along, have me stand near what I build, take pictures. They jus' despise that. Many people have told me they didn't understand it. But puttin' it in newspapers, it's jus' beginnin' to show it better than what they thought it was, and now they're jealous and have hatred and dislike on account of it. It jus' turned out a little better than they thought it was.

[The people here] still don't accept it. Seems like all the business I get sellin' this stuff is to far away places. Nobody around here don't want to have anything to do with what I'm doin.' They call it junk, that mess. [They] suspicion I drink a little beer after ever what money I make. I drink a little beer. Many of them say, "He don't get any of my money to buy beer with or to get drunk off of." The way I react a lot of times is I go and buy beer and mess and I come back here. I call this the bunk house.[8] I come back in here and I drink beer and I look at a piece of wood. I relax and let it come out. I get head strong and I go out and take the hatchet, and actually I knock it out. I can do it without drinkin' beer, but I jus' let beer be a part of it. Everybody have their own way of doin' things, have their own likes.

I used to be bad about drinkin' liquor, but I got where I can't keep it on my stomach. Beer is milder and softer than liquor. I lost my license on account of drinkin' alcohol. You learn from mistakes, you know. My brother buys corn flakes. He bought corn flakes and bought corn flakes, mostly on Fridays and Saturdays. He wouldn't eat them before dinner during the week, jus' something on week-ends. One day I run across a corn flakes box, had a Statue of Liberty on it. I kept watchin' it. I said, "I believe I'll take a shot at it." And I built a Statue of Liberty. My style of doin' it, I jus' see how to do it. I can see how to do what I want to do. I jus' see it. I don't care what it is. If somebody says, "Build something for me." They tell me in their way of speaking, and I jus' see how to do it.

[To build a concrete figure] you make up in your mind how you want this man to be. Rig this [chicken] wire, then wrap small pieces of wire around. Then you go to a real rough ragged coat of concrete and let it dry. Then you come back along with a finishin' coat to make it look like clothes or whatever. I can do a whole lot better than what you see here, but it takes strong concentration. You don't want a lot of people botherin' you.

---

7 Of his parents' house

8 Jeff's workshop behind his parents' house

Jeff Williams

I've always been interested in signs. [When] I go places or somewhere, I see different accents in signs. I'm jus' really interested in the art world. Sign paintin's an art, jus' as well as sculpture, paintin' portraits. I cut out what I'm goin' to cut out. I take my new machine I bought and smooth it. Ever' once and awhile, I run across a piece that I feel I'm goin' to leave this natural[9] but I have real bad habits of paintin'. I love to paint. Ever' once in a while I leave something natural.

Lately I been using latex [paint] because it dries quick and soaks into the wood. It stays in the wood for a certain length of time. Oil paint [has] a glossy look. It's too update or new lookin.' I like that sort of dull, maybe folk art look.

I like to use sweet gum [wood]. It's tough stuff. Sweet gum is very tough. It agrees with weather a lot. If you got a piece out in the weather, all the cracks heal, close up. Sweet gum is, to my opinion, like a human type of wood. When the rain hit it, you don't see no cracks. The sun hit the piece for two or three days, it cracks, but it be little ol' hair cracks. It never be great big. Something like pine would be an inch crack or 3/8's or quarter [inch] crack. It busts open, so to speak. Sweet gum keeps itself together. I'm a sweet gum freak. I like the smell of it. Termites don't bother sweet gum. It'd take a number of years, a good while, to rot. It don't jus' fade away. Termites eat the hell out of a piece of pine. Juniper and cedar would be good wood to carve out of. But hardly ever you see a tree big enough to carve. Juniper and cedar is a real light wood. It's not real heavy. Sweet gum is heavy.

When I carve a piece, I have an expression, like black or white. The shape of the wood, a lot of times, shows me do I want to make a white man [or a] black man, Puerto Rican, alien, whatever. I have an idea of what I want to make first.

In past years, I've [wanted] to build a man [with] an antique-like look, a horse or jackass with long ears, a man sittin' in a buggy in the old style. I always wanted to build this Roman, that guy with the steel hats that fights with swords [and] have those big round things, shields. If you go to something like that, it really tells a story. If you're really interested or if you pass the test, go into the world of art and build something like that and build it classic. That would really bring out the art in your work. You wouldn't do it in a week. That would look good in concrete. I love the looks of white cement. I want to use [it] sometime. That white cement has its own taste, its own style. It speaks for itself.

My goal is to stay in the art world. Something I want to do. I love to use the cuttin' saw. I like to use the brush. I like designin' [and] doin' pin strippin' like for cars. I really do want to make

---

9 Unpainted wood

a livin' at carpentry or sculpture. Sculpture work is brain work. You have to really be thinkin'. It's a strain on your brain. Say you're buildin' a flower or doin' some sculpture work with flowers involved — that wouldn't be too simple. It's workin' —hard workin'.

I would love to say, if I would get lucky enough to find a few dollars and build my own style of house. I'd love to start off buildin' a house that looks like a 'bacca[10] barn, then go from there. It would be cheap, the way I'd build it. It wouldn't cost so much. To my opinion, I have my life kinda drawed out, the future. I like antique cars, I like to rig antique cars and make them look my style.

First chance I get, get out of Salemburg. That I'm goin' to do because people's too connivin.' They're not use to what I'm doin.' I'd heap rather be somewhere near sensible people and somebody that's interested in my style of work, be livin' somewhere like that. [Salemburg's a] dry Southern town, kinda lost place, lost people, a lot of murderers, back-stabbers, poor people.

This is my life-style, this is my accent. I love to be around decent people. I love people that's not stupid as hell, picky. I love decent-like type people that I can get along with. I'm the type of person that don't have to be carryin' a big knife or havin' a lot of hatred. I jus' want to keep my mind a free accent. I jus' like decent people.

I could be livin' in New York if I wanted to. But New York is dog-eat-dog, violent people, thieves. What's yours don't belong to you really. The people in upstate New York are like beggars. They'll steal your belongings, then want to tangle with you about your belongings. They's a lot of sick people in New York. They take short cuts in living'.

I'm jus' me. I don't have nobody but me. I runs around a lot and I go places when I want to go. I'm jus' really enjoyin' myself. I'm not married. I don't have no special girlfriend. Jus' me. I do anything.

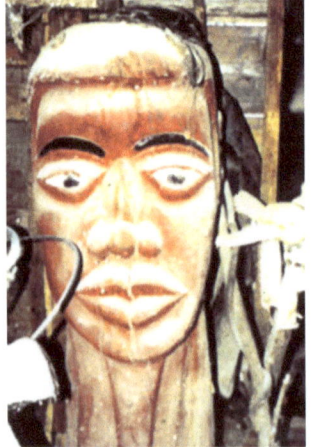
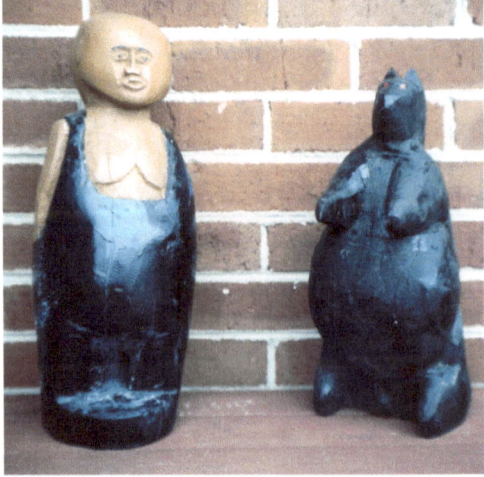

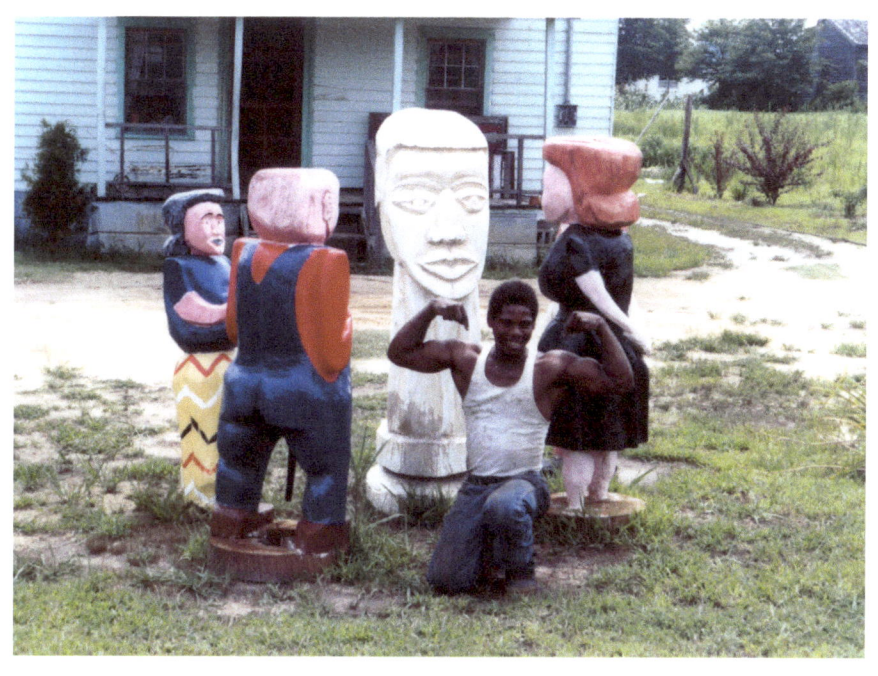

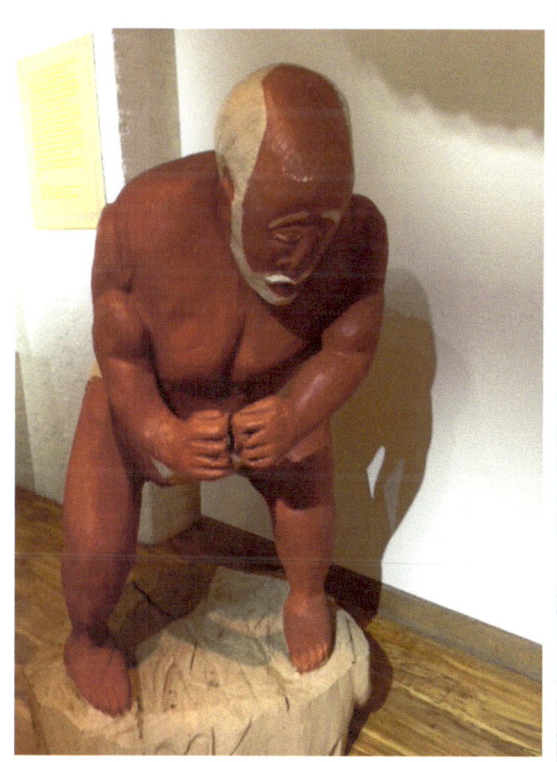

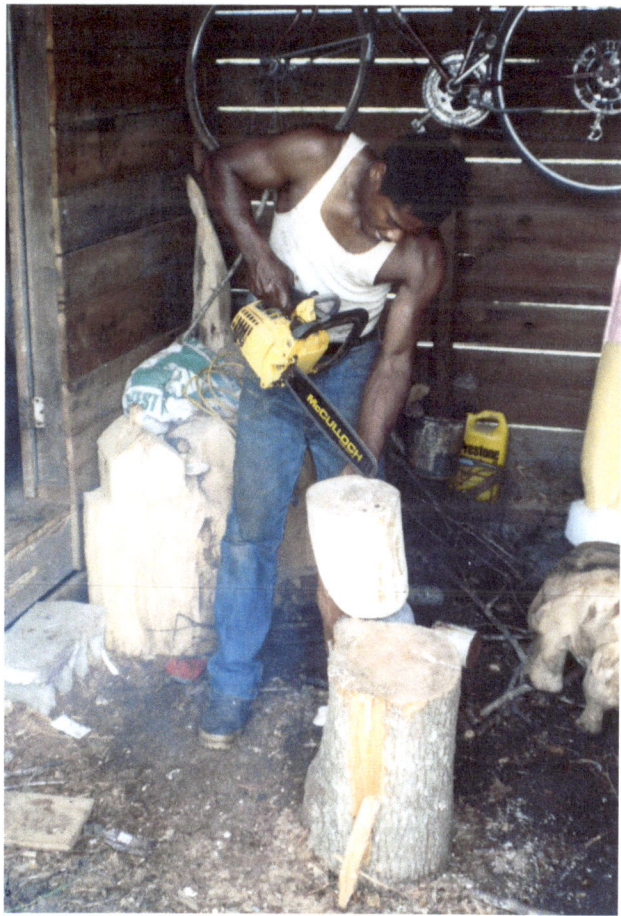

Quinton J. Stephenson (1920 - 1997), self-taught naturalist and sculptor, was recognized by the Smithsonian Institute for his fossil expertise. He constructed and heavily decorated the Occoneechee Trapper's Lodge. The Lodge served as a museum of natural history and was visited by many school children. He created sculpture of prehistoric animals from objects found in the area.

> *I could see these twisted vines in the woods and made a note that I wanted to cut them and make something out of them.*

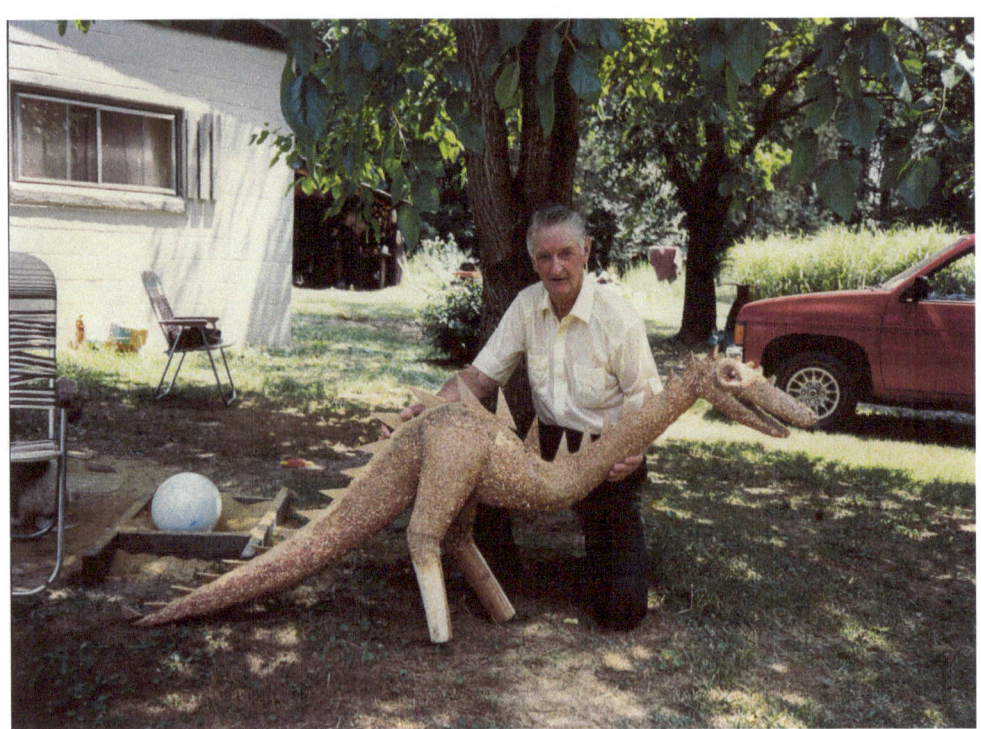

Interviewed in Garysburg, NC: August 20, 1988

Q. J. Stephenson

Q.J. Stephenson – Naturalist and Sculptor

[I was born] 1920 [in the house] right across the road. I had two brothers and two sisters. [My dad] was a travelin' salesman, goin' to different cities. But I was brought up in the depression years and at that time my daddy didn't have a job, and everything was bad. I would roam the woods and fields and work on the farm.

[I started trappin'] in the depression years; in fact, I fed my family off that. All the years I did it, I never went over ten miles from the house. [I trapped mink, muskrat and raccoon. Sears Roebuck paid $1.60 per muskrat fur, compared with the 75 cents a day a man could earn farming.][1] When you live through years that hard, you learn how to succeed.

I never went but to eight grades [in school], but when I was 17 years old in the Civilian Conservation Corps[2], I was sent to a Northern California camp – a forester camp. The boys fought forest fires, built trails right on the Oregon border. We were three miles back off the highway. The most beautiful country in the world, right in the heart of the red wood. Out there, I think, is where I really got interested [in nature]. I visited a lot of the old gold miners and learned a lot about pannin' gold and rocks and stuff. I really got fascinated with the west at that time. I stayed a year.

I came back, [but] I was not home a year before I was drafted into the Army and sent back to California near Death Valley to take desert training. [Then I was sent] to the aircraft factory and I was lucky. We had the big anti-aircraft guns. We was surrounding Los Angeles, 60 miles out. Anti-aircraft outfit.

[After the war I came back to North Carolina.] We had a big gravel pit in Garysburg at that time. I got a job [there]. They run the gravel through a screen, washed it and these big pieces of rock – as big as your head, they would throw them away. I kept watching the rocks and ever' once and a while I would see this petrified wood in them. Nobody else knew what petrified wood was around here. I started savin' the specimens. [That wood] probably grew up in Canada or New York State or somewhere like that. I guess I really became interested right there at the gravel pit.

Later I went into construction work. I moved about in Virginia and North Carolina. Jobs didn't last too long. I got a chance to go into the earth in different spots throughout the coastal plain and piedmont. With a construction company, I run a crane with a drag line. My whole life

---

1 From an article in the News and Observer, December 15, 1991
2 A public work relief program, part of the New Deal, 1933-1942

was digging in the earth and I took an interest in the earth. Most operators would not take an interest in something like that.

That's when I really learned something about the earth, by digging deeper and deeper. Each layer is like another chapter of a book[3]. I learned that the ocean had been over the earth three times; not once, but three different times through this section. Then I started getting help from the Smithsonian Institute. Some of my early finds I donated to them - [there] was a walrus tusk that I dug up[4]. Then I started getting a lot of help about identifying and stuff like that.

[I been married] to Eloise about 40 years. [We have] four children – one boy and three girls. One of my daughters is interested in [rocks and fossils].

All but the winters I was in the Army , every winter , I went [trappin']. In construction I couldn't work one month and a half in the dead of winter – December and part of January. That is all [my trappin'] lasted. I was able to catch enough muskrats to get by during those months. In the winter I [don't] use my canoe. Most of the time I wear waders and walk. I see the signs - like little roots they break and eat and stuff like that. I go by that more than tracks. Most places you can't see a track if it's muddy. I use underwater traps. [Muskrats swim into them head [first] and it kills them outright.

I've had quite a few experiences out there. I was trappin' in a section that I had never been before and it was between two huge hills. A ground hog don't like to get his feet wet. Beavers had built a dam between one hill to the other hill and across the gully. The top of the beaver dam was about eight inches wide. I started down the hill on one side, on the left side. On the right side was a groundhog. He was right on top of the dam on that edge, so both of us were in the center of the dam when we met. He got within eight inches of me and stood up on his hind legs and wanted to see what happened. So I only give an inch. I stood there and stood there and that groundhog won't give a foot. He was chatterin' and his teeth was goin' a mile a minute. I know he was cussin' me in groundhog for all he could do, but I stood there 'til I got tired of it and I stepped off to the other side and he went on by. I reckon if I had stood there an hour it would have been the same thing. It beat all I have ever seen.

I started [the lodge[5]] 40 years ago, working on it an hour here and an hour there. I didn't have

---

3 From an article in the *News and Observer*, December 15, 1991

4 Confirmed by the Smithsonian to be four million years old

5 The Occoneechee Trapper's Lodge, constructed of concrete and decorated by Stephenson, served as a natural history museum visited by school children and art enthusiasts.

much time, but I knew what I was going to do all the time. I have no idea [where my idea come from.] I started with cement block, fillin' it with sand. I stuccoed over it. It represents nothing in the United States. It's just my own idea. I haven't finished; I'll be doing this until I die.

This art work has just been a short while – I say seven years ago I started making these creatures. I could see these twisted vines in the woods and made a note that I wanted to cut them and make something out of them. I found some beauties. I cut them and let them cure. When I started, [the] first I ever made was snakes, I reckon about four or five feet long. The vine was all twisted around just like a snake and they did not last two weeks when somebody bought them. I started on those birds and they went the same way.

[I make concrete plaques using] wisteria vines to go around to outline them. [The vine] is twisted in the shape I want it when I cut it. Have to cure that about a year and treat with wood preservatives and stuff like that. It's got aluminum wire in it [so] it won't pull apart. [I] layer one concrete layer at a time, that's why sometimes it takes days to finish a piece. If you had a mold you could just pour it in there, but people buying art don't want anything made out of a mold.

I use a lot of [rocks] from the creek, a lot of fresh water mussels and use a lot of small white [shells]. I used deer horns that hunters give me during the deer season. I can clip those horns like I want them and soak them overnight in half Clorox and half water. The next morning they are a pretty ivory as you have ever seen, just white as snow. It don't just take but overnight to do it. Like I want a tooth for something, about that long – I just soak it and have a pure white tooth – the tip of a deer horn. During my art work everything is used right around here. Once in a while, I might use plastic teeth or something like that, but that would be all.

Sometimes when I am making a piece of cement, [I embed ferns and leaves] in the cement. It's a pretty tough job to tell you the truth. You can't put them in the concrete when you first [mix and] pour it — water rises to the top. You have to wait until it evaporates just about. When I see all the water is just about gone, I press the leaf into the concrete real tight. When I get all my ferns and leaves pressed in there, I come along with a layer of mica, fine mica, and I block stuff in it – mixed together. I sprinkle that over it and I pack it in. The leaves would not show up unless you had something like that. It would all be the same color. If I want to color the leaves, I put coloring in the cement, [but] I don't use paint. Paint won't stay long out in the weather.

[Sometimes I add] shark or whale bone, fossils, [I find] in sea deposits. It will surprise you. You never know what you will find where the sediment from the sea settled – you know, where the ocean went back. I have found alligator scales, stuff like that.

I look for blue clay the first thing. That is the sediment from the sea. Sometimes I can see that in the [creek] bank eight feet up and that is my first clue right there. Then I start digging in the creeks and start finding seas shells and stuff like that. Like I said, much of that petrified wood is never exposed. You have to dig for that. First the pieces are heavy and they fell to the bottom of the stream and got covered up with sand. The sand is covered with water about four foot deep. You got a problem getting it out.

The most beautiful piece I ever made was a fish and I wish I had it back; one of the first pieces that I ever made. I wish I had never sold it. I would say about 50 or 60 pieces have gone out [of here]. That's all has been in the last seven years. I don't know. I hate getting rid of it. For one thing, I just like to do it – just love to do it. [I'm] always interested in prehistoric creatures. [If I can imagine an animal, it probably lived.] They say they lived on earth 300 million years ago, before humans. Stands to reason because it took that much time for the coal and stuff to build up in the earth.

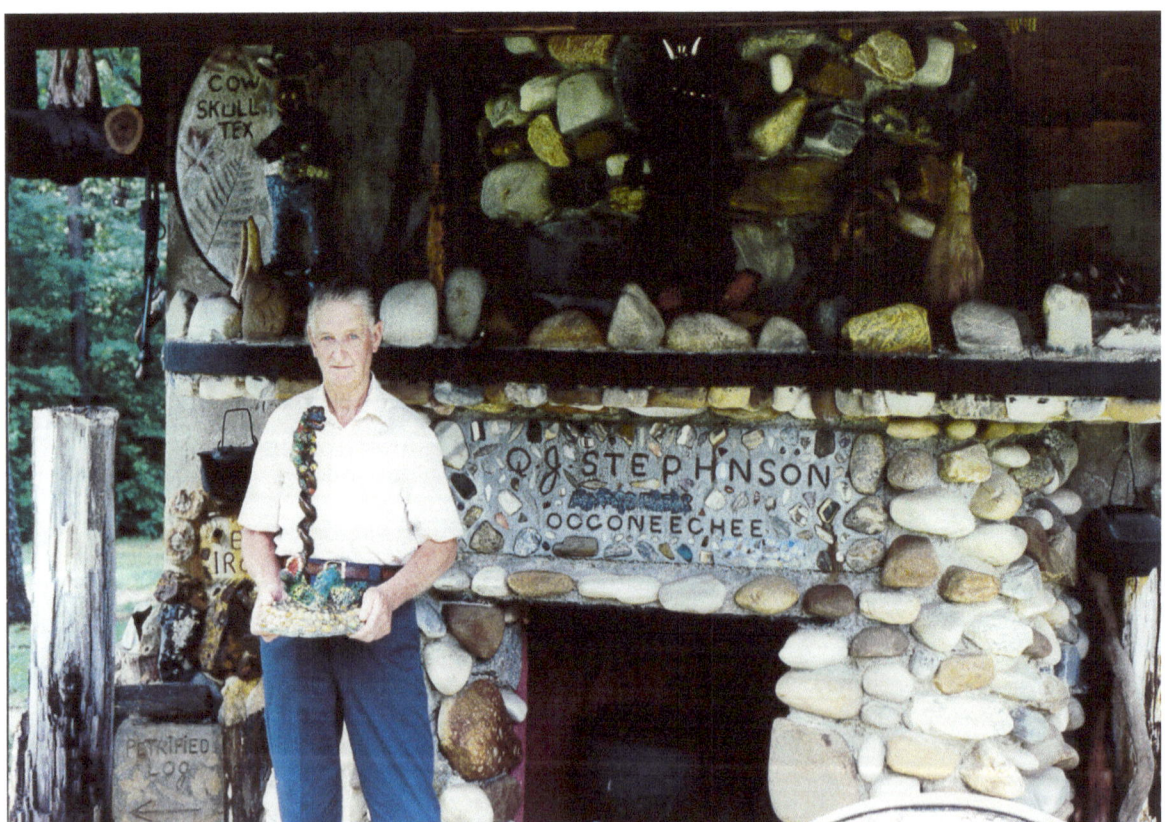

Stephenson at his Occoneechee Lodge

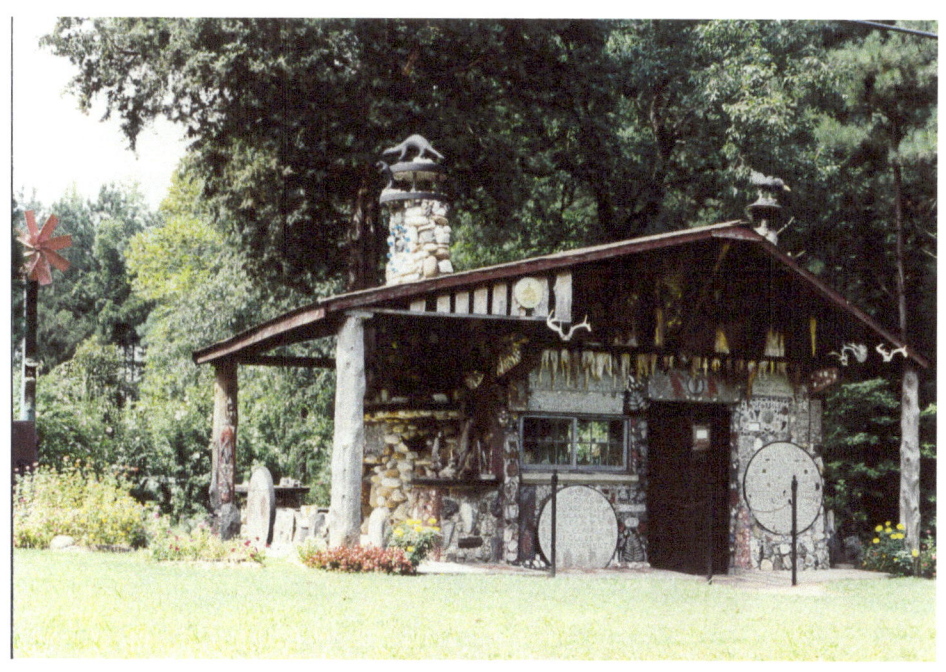

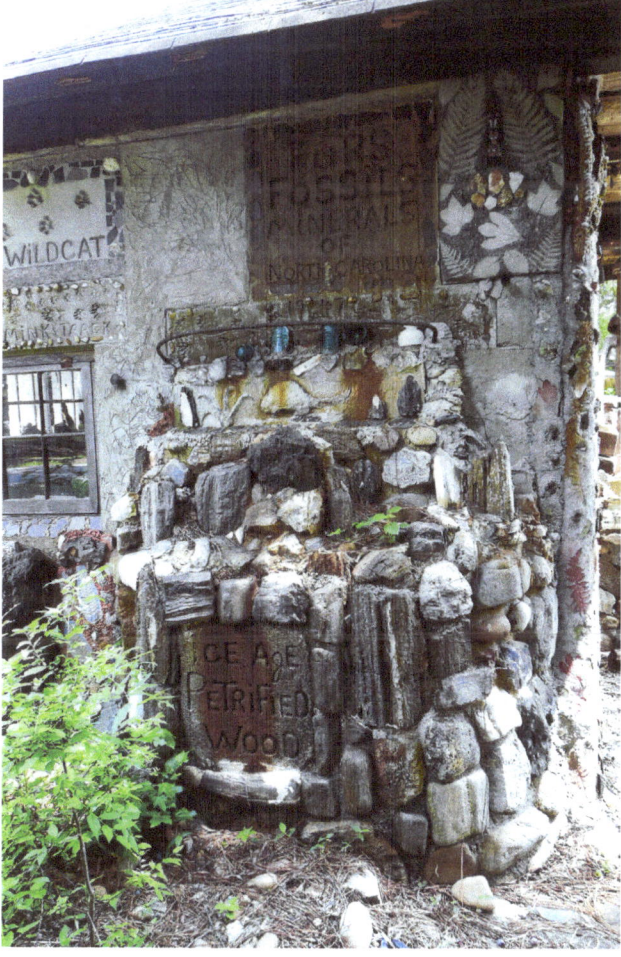

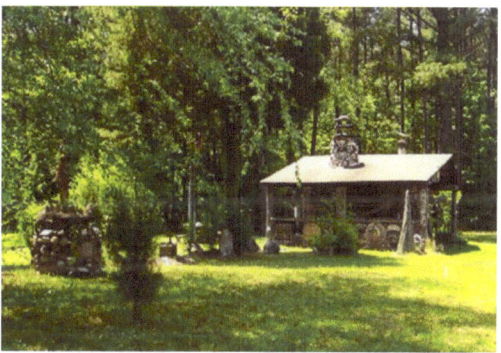

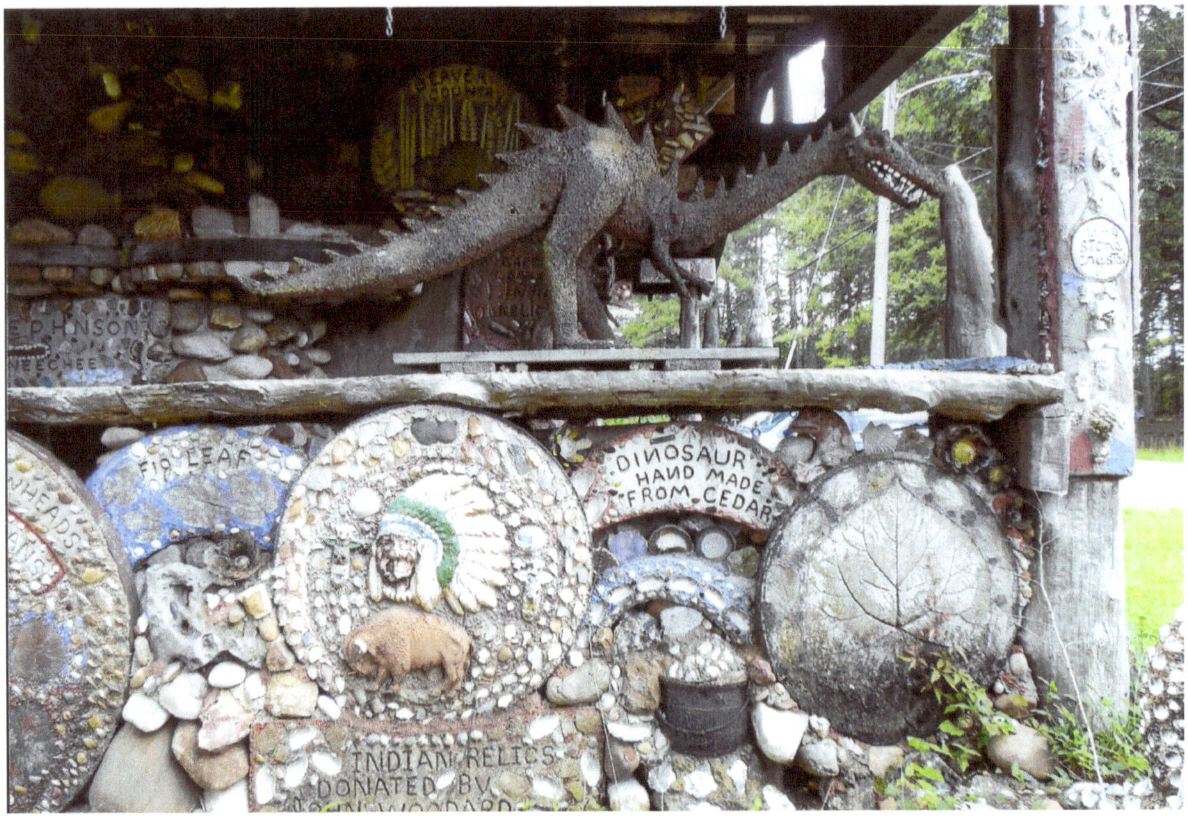

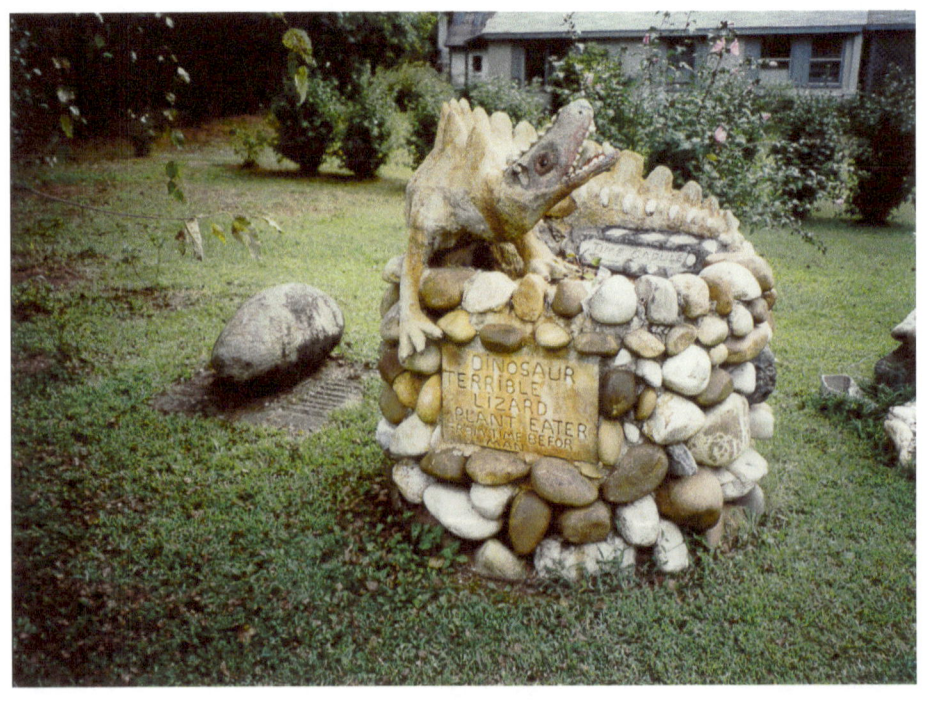

Q. J. Stephenson

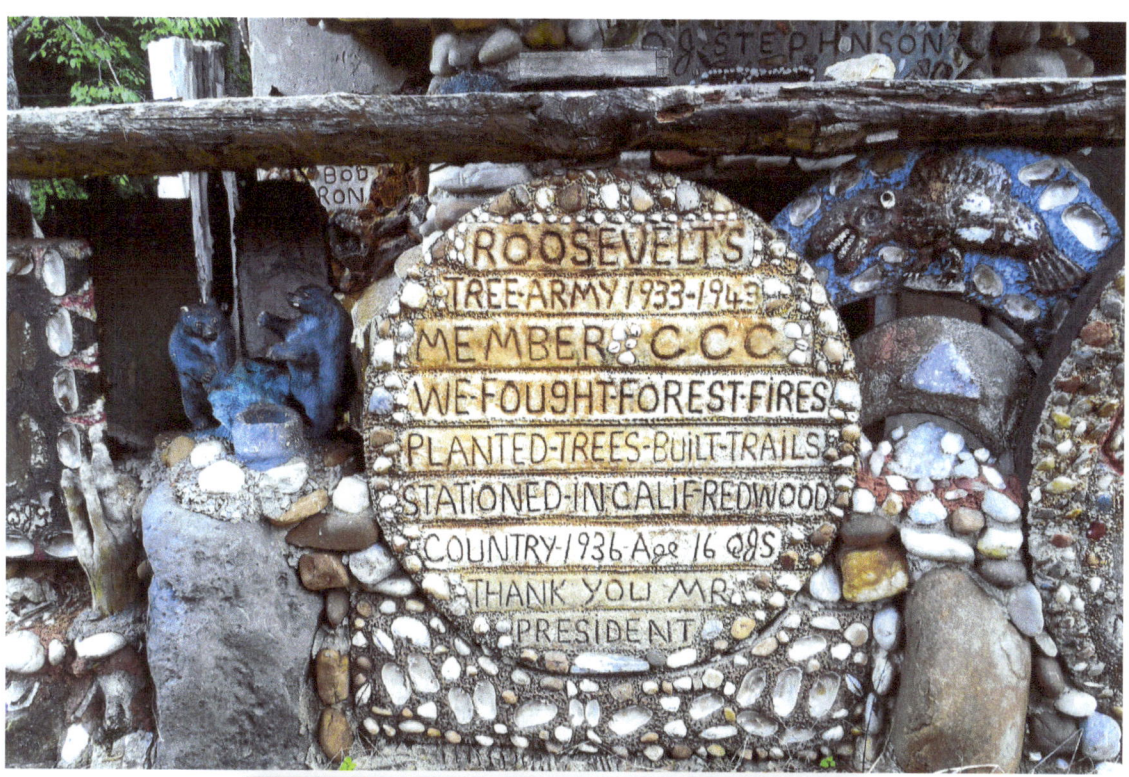

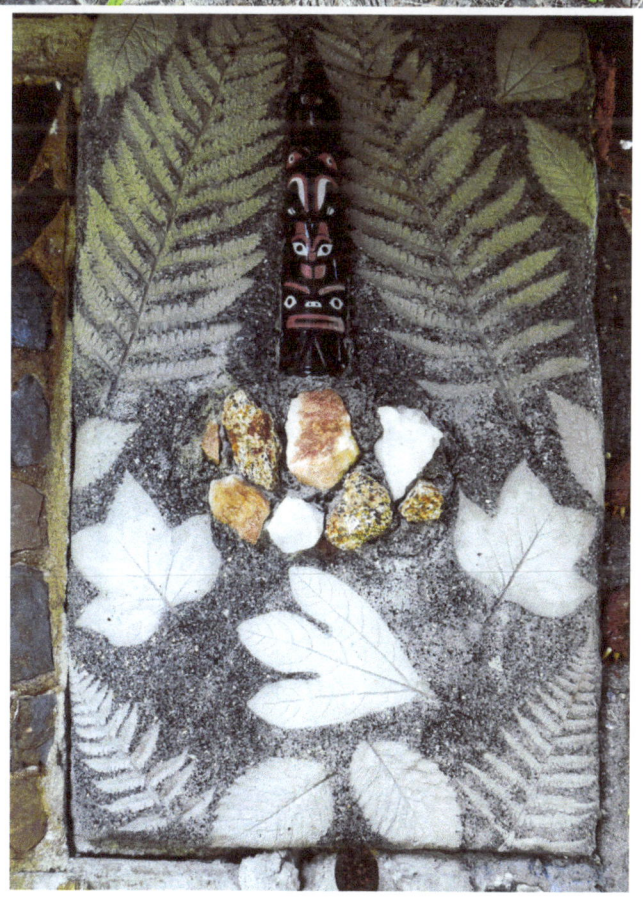

Albert Hodge (1941 -   ) began creating pottery in 1989 when a knee injury forced him to retire from his job as a match cloth cutter for a furniture company. He is a self-taught folk artist who creates his own glazes for each unique piece. One of his trademarks is fiendish faces, with devil horns, china plate teeth, with serpents wrapped around spouts.

I've not had no real help in this; I did it all mostly trial an' error. I'll try somethin' an' if it don't work, I'll keep tryin' until I get it to work. Keep stayin' at it. You never know what's goin' to work for you.

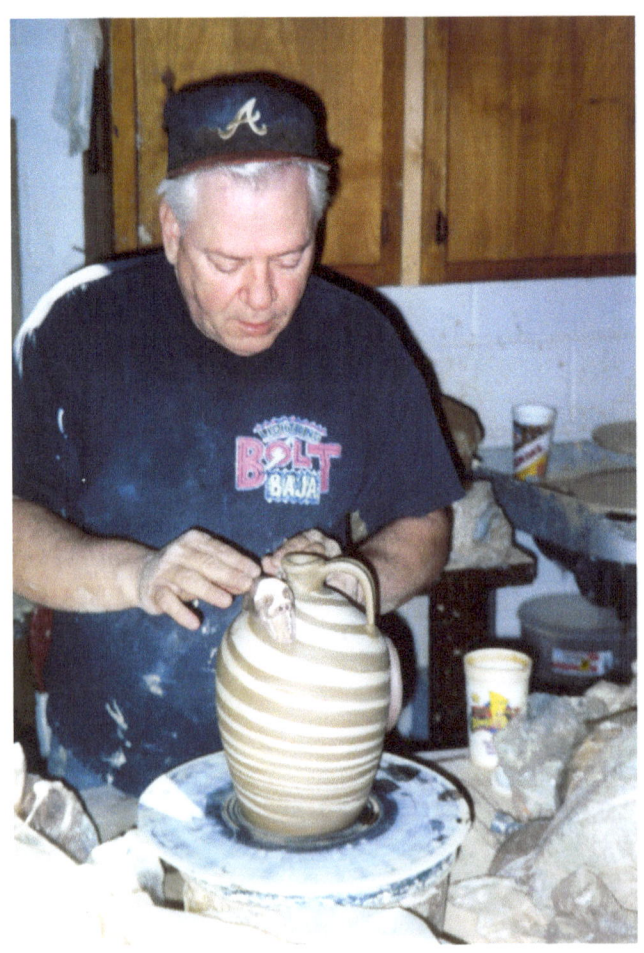

Interviewed in Newton, NC: January 28, 1992

Albert Hodge

ALBERT HODGE - POTTER

Before my momma married my step-daddy, we rented a house right out from the city limits of Newton. They said it was the first courthouse[1] in Catawba County. It was an ol' log house. Me an' my two sisters slept in the loft. We found a snake as long as I am now in our bed one time. It had crawled up the side of ol' house an' come in. There was cracks where the mud came outta those logs, an' when the wind blowed, my God, it would blow the blankets on the bed. We had to stay really close together in the winter to keep warm in that place. You layed right on top of each other. I'd always get in the middle. I was the smallest. I was protected.

People talk about tick mattresses. I went out in the woods many a time, had two sheets sewed together, an' filled 'em with leaves. Used 'em to sleep on. That don't sleep good, an' there's mites in there that eat you up at night. We stayed in that house maybe two years, then we moved into another house [that] had seven acres of land. [The owner] planted five [acres] of cotton. The way we paid the rent on that house was we had to pick five acres of cotton. The welfare or social service department, one of 'em, would come check our house almost ever' week to see if there was groceries for us to eat because there wasn't no man in the house, an' my momma was livin' strictly off welfare, as best I can remember, because she didn't have a job.

The house didn't have no inside plumbin', an' two of the rooms was dirt floors. We had to walk [a quarter mile] to get water. It was an ol' spring. I'll never forget it. Me an' my two sisters would tote that water. I had two little one gallon water buckets that I toted water in. We washed all our clothes in an ol' black pot outside – built a fire under it. Man, it was rough times. Even my sister had to wear my clothes to school. She didn't have enough clothes. She'd wear my clothes, boy clothes, coat an' all. They tried making fun of her, but she whipped ever' one of 'em. They didn't make fun of her long. It was hard.

I can still remember my mother when she was a young woman. God, she was a beautiful woman. She'd put on high heels an' stockin's an' she'd walk down the street in Newton. Back in them days, ever'body'd go to town on Saturday. The streets would jus' be crowded. She'd walk down the street in them high heels an' did that strut, I could see ever'body lookin'. She was a pretty woman. My mother was beautiful. My grandmother was the first Miss Hickory. She was a beautiful woman too. [She's] been a widow 50 years.

---

1   The Mathias Barringer house, home of an early settler of the county

And me, for one, I got shipped off up to the mountains for a year one time. I had to go to school. It was either that, they said, or go to Jackson Training School[2] simply because I refused to hoe cotton. I got mad an' bucked 'em. They said, "We gotta send him off." So they sent me to Crossnore[3]. The only education I ever got was at Crossnore, because when I went to school I didn't worry about doin' my homework or studyin' or anything. All I'd do was fight an' be a tough guy. Because you are what you are. If you come up rough an' tough, that's the way you're gonna be, an' that's the way you're gonna act.

That Crossnore! I hated it when I had to go, but the first report card I got, Pop Jarvis, our house father, told me, "Come back to my room, I want to talk to you a minute." Little did I know what he had in store for me. Hell, I thought he was goin' to kill me. He beat me half to death. My butt was black for a month. That's child abuse, but I'll tell you right now, it worked. I made the best report cards I made in my life from then on. We found out I could study. I brought in all C's an' D's; before it was always straight D's. Unbelievable! He told me, "You bring that report card in here again, there better not be no C's, no D's on it. The only thing acceptable in this dormitory is A's an' B's."

There was about 30 or more of us in that dormitory. We had to work to pay for our keep. The first three months I was there, I had to get up at 4 o'clock every morning an' go down to the mess hall. My job was to make the biscuits. I made 'em by the thousands. Had a big machine, mixed the dough an' all. Then in the afternoon when I came home from school, I rode the trash truck. Every ninety days, your job changed. It was good. I learned a lot. That's where I learned to smoke. We'd go down to the hospital, get all the cigarette butts. It's a wonder I didn't get ever' disease man's ever had. After a winter at Crossnore, I did get a taste of better livin': clean sheets all the time an' regular meals. I kinda took a likin' to it.

I never even seen [my dad] until I was 12. He was a chronic alcoholic, but he was a genius. There wasn't nobody in the world that could play a guitar like him. He could have been famous if he'd lived an' stayed sober. An' he was an interior decorator, an' he was a chef. He had all kinds of gifts, but he died when he was only 40 years old of cirrhosis of the liver. The doctors told him, "You've got six months to live if you keep drinkin'. If you quit it's hard to tell how long you might live because the liver has a way of healin' itself." He said, "I'll just die happy." He jus' kept on puttin' the booze away. I saw him about a year before he died, an' I knowed he had cirrhosis. I asked him why he didn't give it up. He said there wasn't any point.

---

2   Stonewall Jackson Training School located near Concord, NC. A school for troubled boys opened in 1909, the first juvenile detention center in North Carolina.
3   The Crossnore School was established in 1913 as an orphanage and group home.

He'd go up north an' stay a year, then back to Newton for two weeks. He'd stay drunk the time he was here, but when he was up north he wouldn't drink. He had a job at the Carlton Hotel as an interior decorator. At Camp Roosevelt in New York, he was a chef during the summer season when the resort was open. He made tremendous money. He'd come in with a roll of money that would choke a horse. He was big buddies with all the big shots here in Newton, with the millionaires. They all knew my daddy because he was so good at ever'thin'. He was a great [base] ball player when he was comin' up. He could whip anybody that walked. He could whip four or five at a time. It was just nothin' for him to whip a man. He loved to do it.

When he picked a guitar, he could play right along beside the very best in the world, [like] Merle Travis.[4] You couldn't tell him from Merle Travis. He was just that good. He could do virtually anything. You could sit down with him an' talk about baseball. He could go back to a game and recall it play by play, just like he was watchin' it even though that game was played five years back. He could tell you the life history of ever' ball player that was playin' at that time. I still got his ol' portable radio that he took with him ever'where to listen to ever' ball game. He never missed a ball game, didn't matter who was playin'.

He was a great con man. God, he was good. I've even seem him pull his scams. He'd go to Woolworths an' buy these fake weddin' bands an' diamond ring sets. He'd get 'em for $1.39 a set. I've seen him go into a café. He'd take [the rings] an' fold 'em up in a piece of tissue paper an' stick 'em in his billfold. He'd walk right in an' sit down to a total stranger. He'd order up a beer an' sit there an' say, "Man, man, ain't men crazy." The man would say, "Yeah, I reckon' so." "Ah law, I had this little gal, me an' her was goin' to get married. I went the whole length with her. I spent all my money. Bought her this beautiful diamond ring – a karat. Solitary. Now she's with another man. She dumped me. Here I am stuck with the ring. I wish I could find somebody who wanted to bargain. I'd let 'em have it for almost nothin'."

This man sittin' over here's gonna say, "I'd like to see it." An' here he comes. Outta that billfold he slides that tissue paper out, goes through all the motions, an' pulls these babies up. There that big ol' diamond ring a sparklin'. You can't tell 'em from the real thing. The guy picks it over. I can jus' hear this man's mind a goin' right now. "This guy, I'm goin' to get him. I'm goin' to get this off him for nothin'." "What you got in these?" He says, "Well, I gave four hundred dollars for the dern things, but I'll sell 'em cheap. I'm broke an' I've got to get back to New York. I need money to travel." I've seen him get a hundred dollars for a set. An' I've seen him take as little as twenty. But he's not got but $1.39 invested. I've seen him work maybe twenty dummies a day, an' sell ever' one. Serious money. He made big money on them rings.

4   Merle Travis was an American country and western singer.

My daddy had an eye chart. He'd go to Woolworths an' buy all the readin' glasses. He'd buy 'em all. He'd go to the mountains. He'd get out in that rural country, go up to a house. Daddy would say, "Havin' any eye trouble? I'm an ophthalmologist," (or whatever you call 'em). "I'm out on the back roads, jus' startin' out, tryin' to help people in the rural areas. I can give you an eye examination, an' put you in glasses today for such an' such a fee." He would clean them hillsides out, an' come home with more money than you can pack in the front end of a car.

When I came back to Newton I was in the eighth grade. I went back to my old ways real fast. Harvey Lutz was my school teacher. He made a deal with me. If I would jus' sleep an' not bother or disrupt his class, he would pass me. See, I never finished the eighth [grade]; I joined the Army. I was underage when I went in the Army. But me an' him did have an understandin'. I'd stay at the pool room to two or three o'clock ever' mornin'. I'd come home, eat a bite, go to school, then I'd sleep all day in school. What made it so simple was I joined the National Guard. Me an' a couple of buddies wanted to have a little extra money. My company commander jus' happened to be my eighth grade teacher, Harvey Lutz. Then they had a program in the Guard where you could go active. I went in for six months, an' I liked it. You could extend it to 24 if you wanted to stay. So I went ahead an' shot for 24. Got that behind me.

I was right at nineteen when I came back [from the Army]. I went in with a guy over here in a pool room in Newton. He an' I started fightin' chickens. At the time, I was lean an' mean. I lifted weights, did push-ups ever' day. I had chips on both shoulders, an' I really did think I was the baddest thing that ever lived.

I went to jail twenty-eight times for assault 'til I got married. The judge told me, "Man, you're wearin' us out over here." Ever' time I turned around I was in [jail], maybe two or three times in a week. Jus' anybody that wanted to go out on the sidewalk an' slug. I'll tell you what I was doin'. Did a lot of drinkin' back then. I'd buy a case of beer ever' day. A case a day. Well, I owned part of the pool room. We was makin' pretty good money fightin' chickens, an' even had a poker house up in the top of the pool room. We ran poker games. I had plenty money comin' in, [but] I was payin' it all out for court fines for fightin'. Back then, all they charged you was $15.40 for court costs. But I had so many suspended sentences, they was overlappin'. If they'd ever sent me off for the ones I had, I'd probably still be [in jail] today. I had a wild disposition, an' it come from a rough upbringin', by golly.

I met Peggy when I was about twenty. Her momma an' daddy; they was so scared. I was in the pool room fightin' chickens like crazy. A buddy of mine was datin' her girlfriend. He said, "Do you want to go to the drive-in?" I said, "I don't know." He said, "Well, she's got a girlfriend – right cute. You might like her." I said, "Well, I ain't got nothing else to do." I went with him an' the girlfriend was Peggy.

Peggy was real young. It was her first date, an' she slipped out to do it. Her momma an' daddy, later on, found out that I was seein' her. I dated Peggy four months before I married her. It was a short relationship. It was a nightmare for her momma an' daddy. The district attorney in Newton at the time, he knew me. I'd built myself up a reputation in Newton as probably the wildest man in the country, an' probably faced the judge more than anybody in a short length of time for all the hell raisin' an' drinkin' an' fightin' I done.

The sheriff of Catawba County an' [the district attorney] went down to Little Mountain an' paid my mother-in-law an' daddy-in-law a little visit. They asked 'em if they knew anything about me. They said they didn't. They said, "Well, we feel you should know about this man your daughter is keepin' company with." When they got done tellin' my in-laws about me, it scared 'em within an inch of their lives. Then when I went by to visit Peggy, they told me straight up that they didn't want me to ever come there again, an' if I did, they'd have me locked up for trespassin'.

Bein' the animal I was, I didn't take that too easy. I didn't like it. I was not goin' to let 'em keep me away from Peggy. By that time I already knew I was goin' to marry her. There wasn't no way outta it. She was mine. I sure wasn't goin' to let 'em stand in my way. They found that out to be true.

I had my buddy an' his girlfriend go by an' pick Peggy up. I was layin' down in the back seat of the car. We went to the drive-in, came back, an' I layed back down in the seat. We let Peggy out, went on an' left on our merry way. I know they didn't know I was in there. Somehow somebody must have seen us an' told her mamma an' daddy that I was hid in the car. Her momma goes to the courthouse an' has a warrant taken out for me trespassin'. Yeah! I told Mrs. Drum, "I know they talked to you. I ain't no bank robber; all I've done is fight. I hadn't really done anything bad." She said, "You'll never marry my daughter. [She'll] not marry trash like you. She's goin' to marry somebody who'll amount to somethin'. She'll never have nothin' with you."

Before Mr. an' Mrs. Drum died, before her momma had her stroke an' got bedfast, they came to our house ever' single week. I'd become their favorite son-in-law. Right up until Dad died, he liked me the best; he told me so. It's not braggin'. It's the truth. I went from bein' the one he hated to the one he liked.

Me an' [Peggy] made sure that both our daughters had the best of everything. They had dance lessons; I let both of them join the Y[5]. I worked double jobs to make sure they had the best school clothes. Ever'body in school thought they was rich when they was really poor.

I had a rule about report cards. I made sure they brought home a good one home. I seen what happened to me by not studyin'. I'm dumb right today. I can't write what I want to because I jus' can't spell. It's jus' plain an' simple. I can't read as good as I need to be able to read, an' it's my own fault. I let school go. I didn't think I needed it. Well, I know I need it now, but it's too late. It's hard to teach an ol' dog new tricks. Don't think I didn't try.

When my kids started school I said, "Well, this is my chance to start school all over." It didn't work out like that. Number one: I didn't really have the time to sit with 'em that much. When they had problems, me an' Peggy would help 'em. But if they didn't have problems, I was busy workin', makin' a livin'.

I probably worked 75 or 80 hours ever' week I've been married. I've always worked two jobs almost, an' had side lines – swapped, traded, sold, an' done ever' thing you can imagine. The first job I had was sellin' for the Army-Navy store. I learned a lot from [the owner] on short cuts, buildin' my own counters an' ever' thing in that store. I was assistant manager an' I done good. But then I went to Gulf State Paper an' made foreman in less than a year. I was foreman for close to five years. Both my babies was born while I worked there. [I] could run any machine in that plant an' [I] was the mechanic. I was foreman because I could tear it apart an' put it together. I got my hand caught in one of the machines, an' I've got a lot of disability in that hand. [I] left that [job] an' got into cuttin' cloth[6] an' I did that right up until I started makin' pottery.

I did all kind of jobs other than that. I owned the first pet shop in Catawba County, an' me an' Peggy run it for six years on the side. I started it off with $2,500 an' made $1,400 the first weekend I was in business. I had a high class clientele. Then I owned a business on Highway 321 sellin' utility buildings. Then I was part owner in Four Lane Pool Room for a good spell. I sold lightning rods. [I]made as much as $1,000 a day sellin' lightning rods. I've done a lot of sellin': real successful. Made a lot of money.

I've probably made more money off yard sales than most people think could be made. I'd go buy up all the refrigerators, washin' machines an' air conditioners, bring em' home, repaint 'em an' resell 'em. [I] did it for years. I sold 36 refrigerators the last year I sold. I was always swappin' some an' tradin' some. It jus' never ended.

---

5   YMCA
6   Cutting cloth for upholstery in a furniture factory.

Albert Hodge

This pottery business, the thing that got me in it, was collectin' ol' pottery. I started collectin' an' got discouraged because it was too expensive, the ol' pieces. Most of it was brok[en]. I jus' had a gut feelin' that I could make it. I've always been one to gamble. I went out an' bought a wheel never knowin' whether I could make it or not. I was willin' to play out a hunch, an' it's turned out all right.

I bought [the wheel] in July, 1990. That ain't been two years yet. If you stop an' think about it, Burlon Craig was an apprentice probably for twenty years from what I read. Between the three top potters here in Catawba County, they've got over 105 years of experience. I don't have two years. Some people try to measure me by them. I say, "Hey, it's impossible. You can't measure me to these other people. How would you do it? They've got so much time an' grade in, been on the market an' exposed to the public for so many years. Here I am, jus' the new kid on the block an' really shouldn't even be where I'm at. Now if that's not a miracle, what is? Think about it."

When me an' Peggy was coming along, I had ever' hobby you could have. I have crocheted, knitted, made rugs outta loops, potholders, made baskets, oil paintin'. Ever' thing but clay. Jus' never got into clay. Maybe it all goes hand in hand.

As far as the chicken, I was a chicken fighter so I know the body of a chicken. I've held 'em in hand for hours an' hours. I can tell you what a chicken feels like, believe you me. I've felt their heart beat in my hands for hours, an' raised 'em by the hundreds. No big deal.

I used to do carpentry. Used to draw an' paint cartoons. I did a cartoon on a crow called Ol' Bob.

I've done booze an' cigarettes. I've done ever'thing but I've never tried no dope. That's one thing I've been scared to death of. I'm not no athetist; I jus' don't go to church. I know I should, but I jus' don't do it. I've been a member of a church since I was twelve years old, but I ain't been to it ten times in the last fifteen years.

[You ask about] the first pot I made? Well, I've got a Charlie Lisk[7] jug that had a snake on it. I [decided] to make one, [but make] it different: I would put scales on the snake. After [makin' the snake] I tried makin' the jug, but I couldn't. What I made was like a vase, but I put faces on it. I never could figure out how to get the top on it. I couldn't get one up tall enough where I

---

7   Charles Lisk is a well-known Catawba Valley traditional potter.

could collar it in. It took me a long time. Then I saw in that book Turners an' Burners[8] where Burlon Craig was puttin' one together in two pieces so I thought I could pull the bottom half, then pull the top half an' put the two together an' I might have a jug. Well, I did that.

I was collectin' an' bought pottery from Charlie Lisk. I had been to one of his [pottery] sales. [I] went over there an' asked if I could buy some clay, but before I went to Charlie's I had already bought some store-bought clay. I ordered it from Highwater[9]. I knew you could buy [pottery] stuff from Highwater. I had seen it in ceramic books. That's where I ordered my wheel too. [Now] I buy all my clay from South Carolina.

I went to Charlie's an' watchin' him is like watchin' a magician. I watched Charlie turn two different times, maybe 15 minutes each time. I picked up some of the finer points about centerin' up the clay. But Charles Lisk centers the ball of clay on that wheel so fast, he don't know how he does it. You can go over there right now an' watch Charlie an' you won't learn one bloomin' thing [about centerin']. One time you know jus' a couple of principles about makin' pottery, you can make pottery. Number one: if you can center a ball of clay on a wheel, then you whupped half of it. It looks like it would be simple: not so. I didn't think I would ever get a ball of clay centered on that wheel. I would fight, scream, an' melt it down to where I would have nothin'. I could start out with three pounds of clay an' maybe end up with one. Hell, it was a struggle! An' too, I didn't have enough strength in my arms an' hands to hold it where I could center it. An' I was as strong as a bull, but I didn't have the right muscles. I had to develop 'em.

Then I had to learn to pull it up: nobody to show me. I watched Charlie bring it up. He's got this finger he hooks to the bottom of the clay on the outside an' he brings it up. I have never yet pulled a piece like he pulls it. I tried an' it jus' whips it right off the wheel. I had to come up with my own technique of pullin' that clay up. I use the bottom of my hand instead of my finger. The problem is I'm left handed. I want to do ever'thing with my left hand, yet I'm workin' on a right hand wheel. Charlie does his pullin' from the outside of the pot; I do my pullin' from the inside of the pot. It's jus' in reverse. It's kinda crazy, but you get a different result.

I know that's why my swirl[10] is so much different than ever'body else. It is so different it looks fake. But if you watch me turn it, you know the swirl's in the clay. The way it turns out, it's too

8   *Turners and Burners: The Folk Potters of North Carolina* by Charles G. Zug, University of North Carolina Press, 1986.

9   Highwater Clay Company in Asheville sells clay and pottery supplies.

10   Swirl is a decorative element achieved by layering light and dark clays in a pattern and pulling the clay up to create a swirling design on a vessel.

true, it's too true. I wish I could get it to where it'd be messed up[11]. Really, it'd probably sell better, but I don't know how to change it. I guess they'll have to say in history, "the man that made swirl that looked fake."

In the beginning Charlie wouldn't give me [a glaze] recipe. He sold me a five gallon bucket of glaze he made. He said it ought to last me six months. Well it didn't last no time because I had already started goin' crazy makin' pottery. I told him one day, "That glaze, Charlie, I don't like it; it's too brown. I've never seen pottery look like that." So he said, "I'll give you something to put in it that'll darken it up." He gave me a pound of blackbird clay. He said, "mix a little of that in it an' it'll change the color."

I bought three different glaze buckets from him, five gallons to the bucket. I told him, "It'd be a whole lot easier if I made this up myself instead of comin' over here. If you was to die, I'd be in trouble. I wouldn't know this recipe. You gotta tell me what the recipe is." So he said okay, an' he wrote it down. It was real simple. So I got real serious about color. I knew all I had to do was play with clays an' I could come up with different colors. I got on the phone with Highwater an' ordered all kinds of clay an' I mixed glazes. I come up with some I like, like that molasses color. The honey color, I come up with that. I make my own cobalt colors. The clear [glaze] I got from a recipe book.

The recipe [Charlie] gave me, if I had knowed it, I could have got out of the local library because that recipe was used by the Chinese back in 500 BC. Same identical recipe. I thought it was the Catawba Valley glaze. I thought Burlon Craig an' all of 'em had a secret recipe. Well, the Chinese had it for thousands of years: the ash glaze. I finally did get me a book on glazes an' I've used it to help myself some. My stuff's startin' to look better.

I've not had no real help in this; I did it all mostly trial an' error. I'll try somethin' an' if it don't work, I'll keep tryin' until I get it to work. Keep stayin' at it. You never know what's goin' to work for you.

---

11 Albert's swirl has tight, demarcated lines of clay, rather than dark and light edges that bleed into one another.

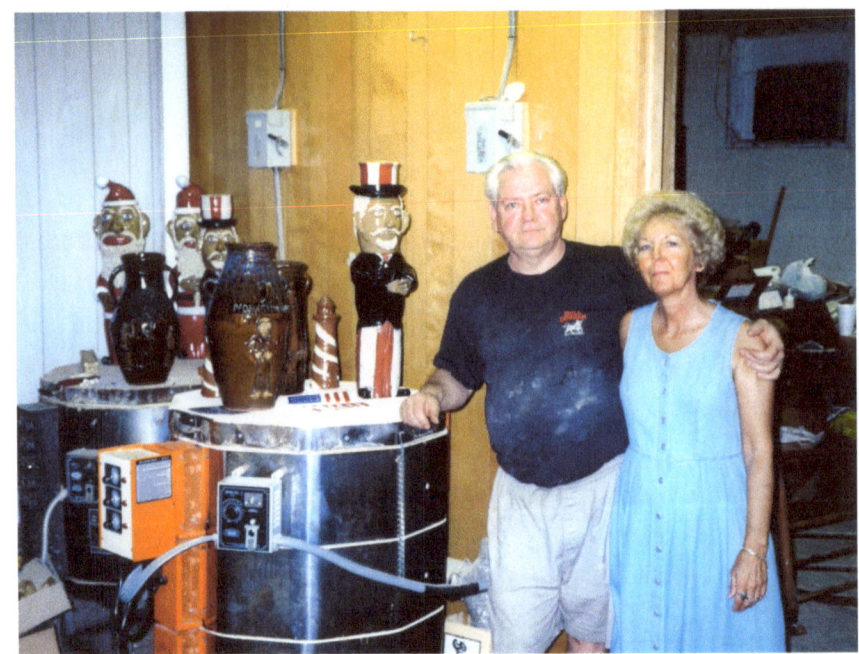

Albert and Peggy Hodge, 1998

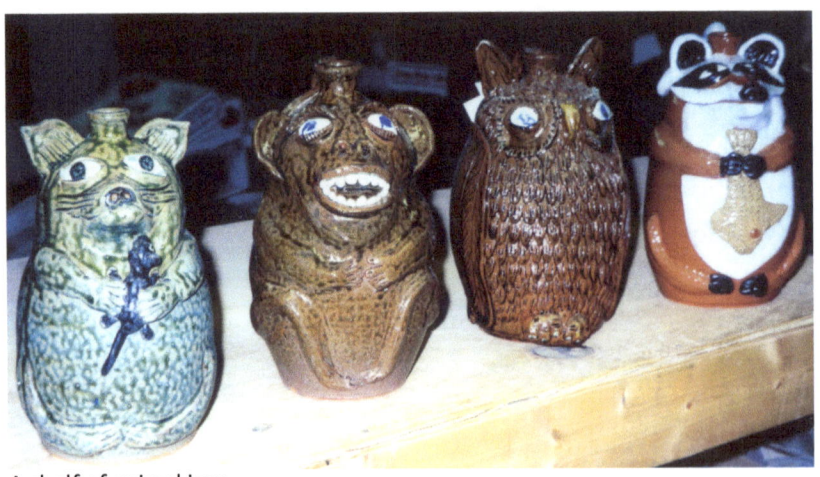

A shelf of animal jugs

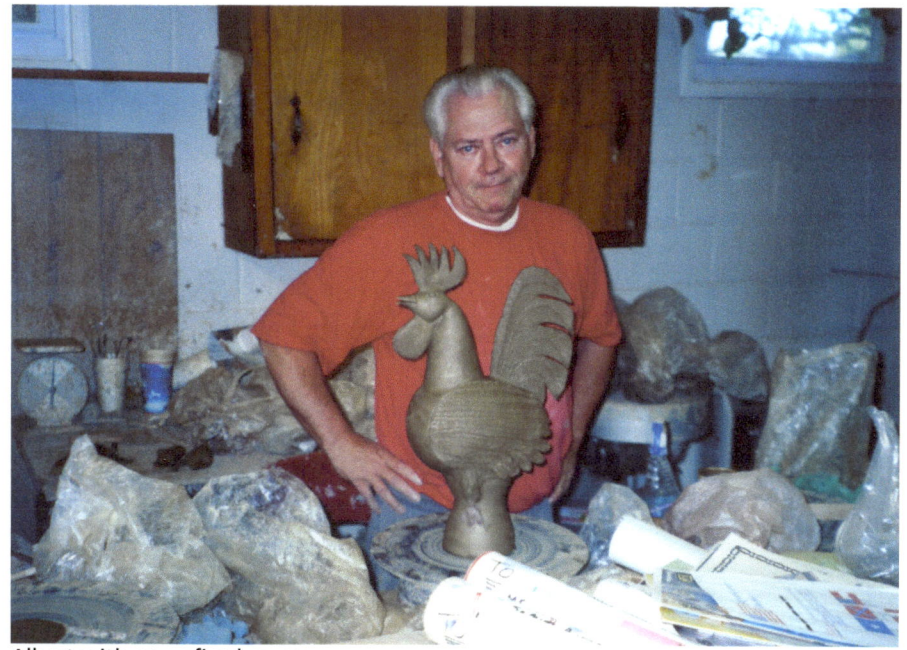

Albert with an unfired rooster

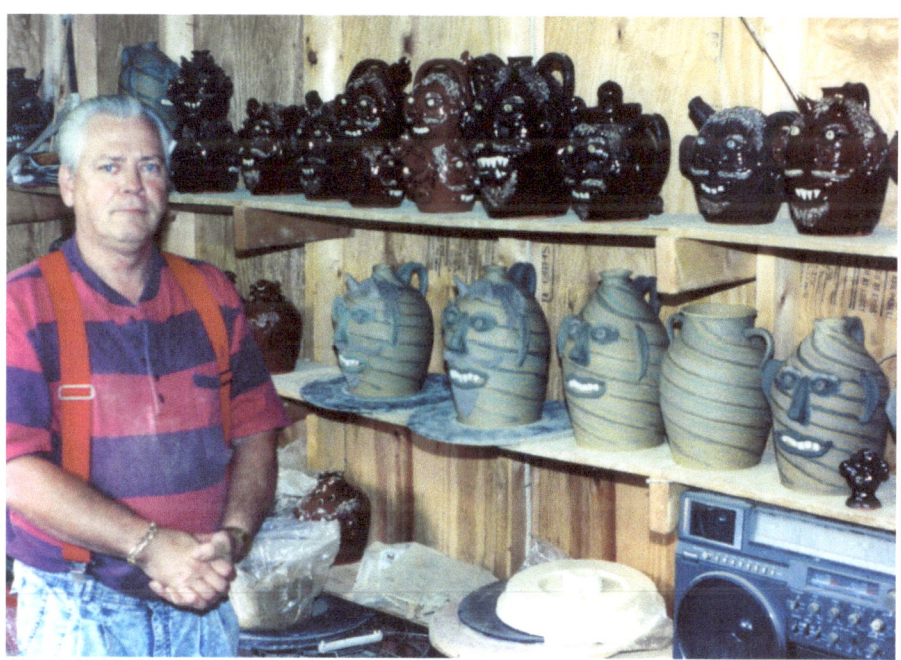

Albert in his shop

ABOUT THE PROJECT

When undertaking this project in early 1980, I envisioned interviews accompanied by photographs and collaborative paintings of the artists.

Minnie Reinhardt painted the small pictures on her wall in my painting of her at work, which I chose for the cover of this book. James Cook carved the border of the block of wood I supplied and I used it to frame my painting. I added the little seashell Elenora Hamiltion decorated to my painting of her house and the Island.

My idea was not very practical and I abandoned it when challenged by potter's clay. The series is not complete but I have a canvas with a border painted by Jeff Williams. Thirty years have passed. I have placed the series on my list of things to do.

~ Barry Gurley Huffman

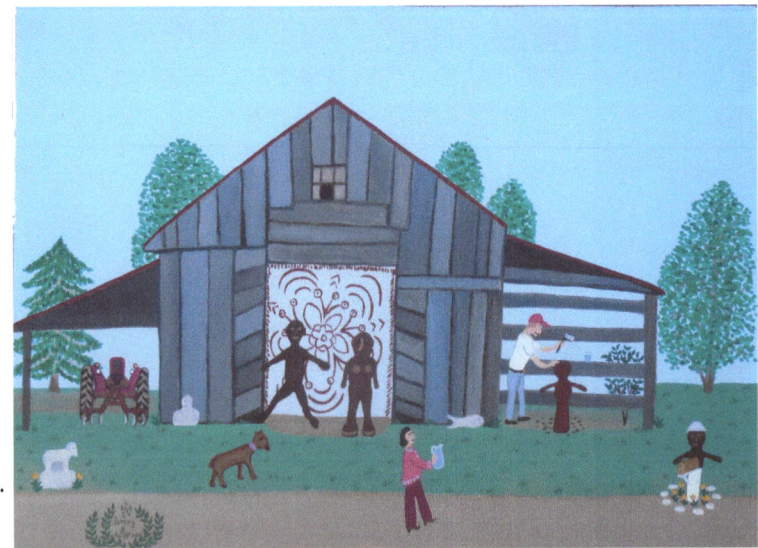

Raymond Coins Works in His Barn. 1984.
Ruby Coins takes water to her husband.

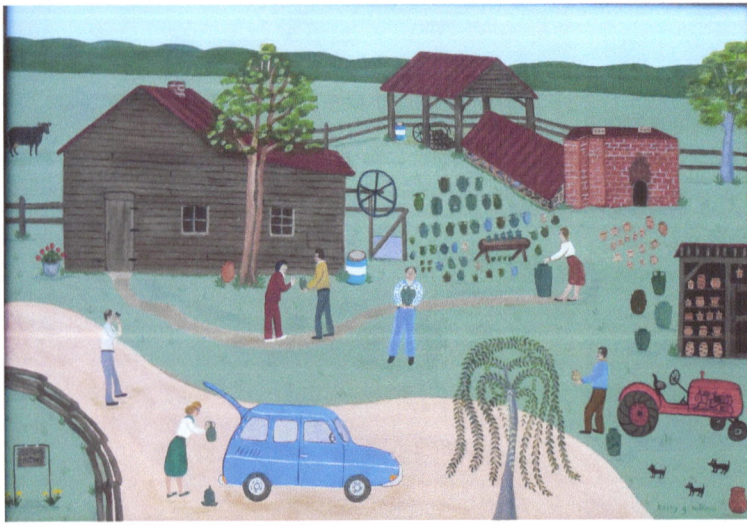

Kiln Sale at Burlon Craig's Pottery. 1980.
I am putting a piece of pottery in the car,
Allen is taking a photograph, and Irene
Craig is helping a customer.

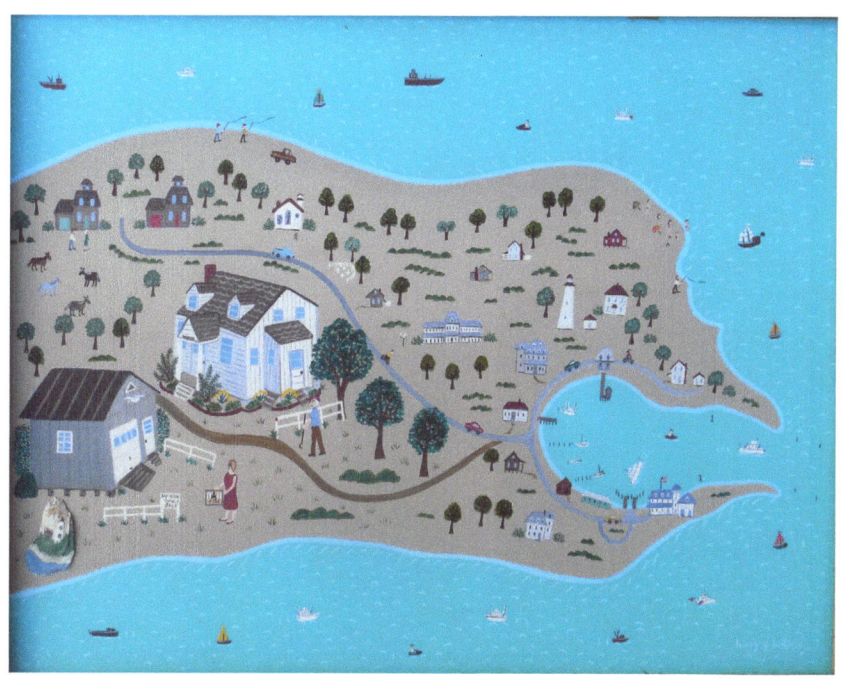

Elenora Hamilton at Home on Ocracoke Island. 1983.
Mrs. Hamilton painted the small seashell located under the garage. She painted small items to sell in her garage shop.

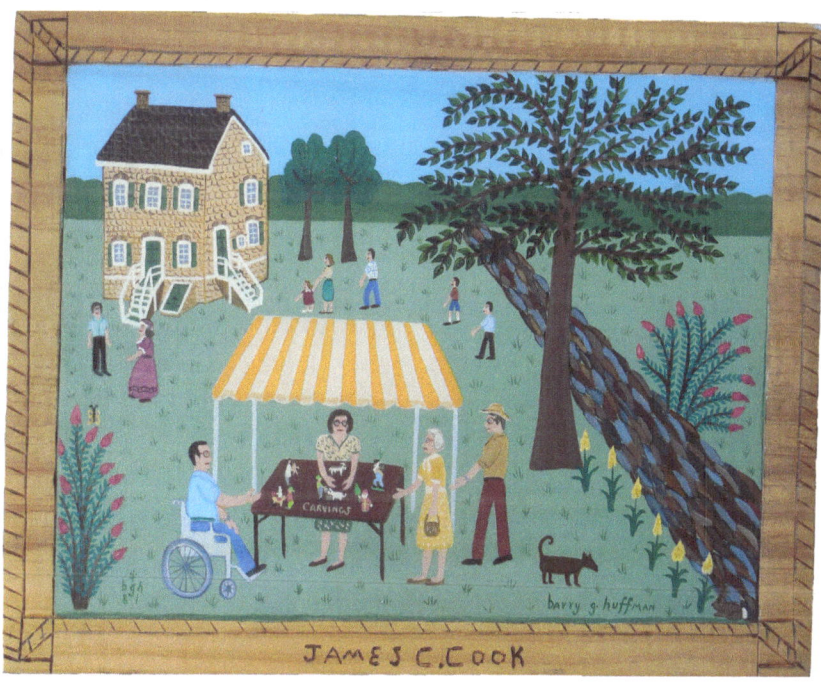

James Cook at Charlotte's History Museum. 1981.
James Cook carved the border and signed the wood block.

www.ingramcontent.com/pod-product-compliance
Lightning Source LLC
Chambersburg PA
CBHW050853180526

45159CB00007B/2658